PRAISE FOR THE C

Baron is convicting, chall
This is a must-read for the Christian leader who truly desires
to serve God rather than ego, Christian political correctness, or
selfish ambition in their ministry.

—FOLEY BEACH, ANGLICAN BISHOP AND PASTOR

With depth of professional and pastoral experience, Tony
Baron exhorts leaders toward a model of leadership rooted
in discipleship to Jesus. *The Cross and the Towel* is a refreshing
alternative to much of the power-based business practices of
leadership found today. This ancient approach to leadership is as
relevant today as ever. I highly recommend it!

—DR. KEITH J. MATTHEWS
PROFESSOR & CHAIR OF THE MINISTRY DEPARTMENT
GRADUATE SCHOOL OF THEOLOGY
AZUSA PACIFIC UNIVERSITY

Refreshing! Baron prods us to come to our senses about
Kingdom leadership. Among a myriad quantity of self-help
manuals, he yanks us back to first things....

—FRANK LYONS, ANGLICAN BISHOP OF BOLIVIA

Tony Baron is a gifted theologian and a perceptive clinician.
In his most recent book, he has skillfully addressed the crisis
facing contemporary church leadership while offering sound
and practical steps toward a leadership style that seeks to employ
Kingdom principles. This book is a must-read for any Christ
follower who is ready to trade the bankrupt tools of the sword and
the shield for effective leadership tools of the cross and the towel.

—KIRSTEN GARDNER, TEACHING PASTOR
THE WAY CHRISTIAN FELLOWSHIP

In the late 1990s my church sent me to a conference on church growth that was being held at a mega church in Chicago. I went and my eyes were opened to many new ideas, but I came away with the greatest impact from a fellow I ran into in a hallway crowded with people trying to find their next class. He was an elderly black man with a captivatingly beautiful accent. He reached out and held my hand for a moment, looked at me directly with his sad, clear eyes and he said, "The Bride is sick. The Groom is coming soon, and the Bride is sick." Immediately I knew he was right and I wondered if I had met an angel. Those of us who have served as shepherds in one capacity or another are quite aware that there is a great work that needs to be done to restore the good health of the bride... the church. Tony Baron has addressed this in a clear and effective manner, bringing the issues home for those who truly want to get a firm hold on service "on earth as it is in heaven." You will be enlightened and blessed.

—Teresa Goode
Fellow Child of King Jesus

A wise person once told me, "don't pray for more power than you have the character to handle." Tony Baron's new book, *The Cross and the Towel*, will help you get a handle on a kind of leadership that is desperately needed in ministry today. Better than that, Tony has become the kind of leader he writes about and can help transform leaders that are following along with him in the higher calling of Christ's power in ministry.

—Keith Meyer, author of *Whole Life Transformation: Becoming the Change Your Church Needs*

The Cross
and the Towel

Leading to a Higher Calling

Tony Baron

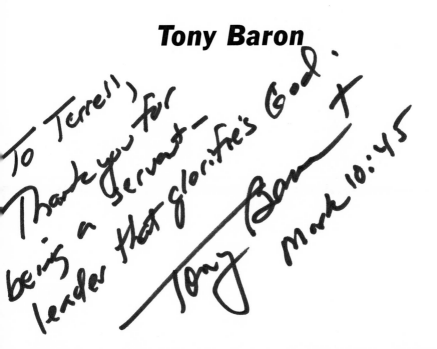

To Terrell,
Thank you for
being a servant—
leader that glorifies God.

Tony Baron
Mark 10:45

The Cross and the Towel: Leading to a Higher Calling

Published by Wheatmark®
610 East Delano Street, Suite 104, Tucson, Arizona 85705 U.S.A.
www.wheatmark.com

ISBN: 978-1-60494-535-5 (paperback)
ISBN: 978-1-60494-536-2 (hardcover)
LCCN: 2010938919

Unless otherwise noted, all biblical citations are from The New Oxford Annotated Bible, New Revised Standard Version. New York, NY: Oxford University Press, Inc., 1994.

rev201101

It is with heartfelt gratitude that I dedicate this book to Dr. Gary C. Stafford, who first taught me what it means to be a shepherd of God's flock, and to all present and future pastors who seek to live their lives according to the cross and the towel.

Contents

PART I THE LEADERSHIP CRISIS:
LEADING WITH THE SWORD AND THE SHIELD

- The Cross and the Towel
- The Cross of Jesus
- The Towel of Jesus
- What's the Difference?

- Positional Power
- Pleasure Principle
- Professional Status
- The Jesus Way
- The Results of Adopting These Symbols of Power

**PART II THE LEADERSHIP SOLUTION:
LEADING WITH THE CROSS AND THE TOWEL**

Contents

PART III THE LEADERSHIP CREED

- Act Strategically
- Encourage Relationships
- Persevere Patiently
- Inspire Responsibility
- Invest in Motivated People
- Acknowledge Pre-existing Problems
- Live for One
- Concluding Thoughts

Foreword

Leadership matters. It sets the vibe in the small household of a single parent. Leadership controls the ethos of all kinds of large enterprises—corporations, universities, and megachurches. And leadership is a difference-maker in all the businesses, schools, hospitals, nonprofits, and families of averaged-sized places of human activity. Leadership is ubiquitous. It surrounds us. It is to us what water is to fish or air is to birds. It envelops and permeates every fabric of our society.

Because the sentences above are true, it is reasonable to assert that leadership, like global warming, war, global economics, and shifting political realities, is presently a primary topic of concern for the whole human race.

This is especially true in current American culture. Recently, because of the mood of deconstruction that swirls around us, many young people—and some boomers in Tony's and my generation—have wondered if we can do without leadership. They wonder if the practices of leadership they have known can be adjusted or replaced, or if leadership as now practiced is so broken, so dysfunctional, so mean-spirited, and so selfish that we would be better off with out it.

I have genuine empathy for the question. It puts a finger on a large and growing problem. Bad leadership is bad for humanity. But the fundamental idea behind the question barks up the wrong tree. It takes the wrong road at the "Y" intersection that lies before us. When it comes to leadership, we have lots of alternatives—but no leadership is not an option. Leaders have always risen. Leaders will continue to rise. We need leadership that comes from leaders who are simultaneously ethical and effective. We need leaders who know both how to love others and move people and enterprises to a preferable future. We do have the option, and the ability, to choose that road.

Happily, you've gotten your hands on a book that gives a way forward. *The Cross and the Towel* shows us how to deconstruct bad leadership. But it does not leave us hanging there—poorer and having lost something of great human value. Rather Tony Baron constructs for us new habits, attitudes, and practices for leadership that are good for everyone: workers, stockholders, customers, vendors, and the observing public.

As you thumb through the table of contents and flip through the pages of this book, your first thought might be, "Duh! There is nothing new here!" That's an understandable reaction. There has been a lot written on leadership in the last twenty-five years. But although the topics might look familiar, the angles and perspectives set forward in this book are fresh. *Fresh,* like we all value in fresh fruit or fresh air.

And besides, the obvious is not necessarily easily applied in real life. The kind of sane leadership we all hope for takes more than mental understanding. It means becoming a different kind

Foreword

of person. *The Cross and the Towel* gives us the vision we need to construct a new leadership reality. It helps us make the necessary choices to embody that reality, and it gives us the means to do so.

If your intuition tells you that leadership is often broken but that we can't do without it—and if you want to be part of the solution—read on. In *The Cross,* you will find a way to die to yourself for the good of others. With *The Towel,* you'll learn the new way of being that you have been dreaming of and hoping could come to pass.

TODD HUNTER
MISSIONARY BISHOP: THE ANGLICAN MISSION
FOUNDING PASTOR: HOLY TRINITY CHURCH, COSTA MESA, CA
AUTHOR: *Christianity Beyond Belief*
Giving Church Another Chance
The Outsider Interviews
The Accidental Anglican

Acknowledgments

It is in prayer that the delicate and delightful relationship between the perfect heavenly Father and the imperfect earthly son comes alive. My prayers have shaped my faith, defined my identity, and clarified my priorities as his servant and as a shepherd to his flock. My prayers have filled me with gratitude for his grace, mercy, and love. They also filled me with gratitude for all the saints he has sent my way to mold me as a writer and a witness to the Gospel message of how to live on earth as it is in heaven.

Thank you to Bobbi, my most precious gift from God. He gave you to me at one of the lowest points in my life. Since we first met, decades have passed quickly, but my heart still skips a beat when I see you. Thank you for being my wife, my ministry partner, and my best friend. You are beautiful, inside and out, my love. Thank you for believing in me and always praying for me.

Thank you to my dear friends, Art and Lori Barter, for their generous support to the ministry of writing and teaching. Their vision to create an organization dedicated to servant leadership has already made a deep impact on the lives of corporate leaders, church pastors, and academic professors. May God continue to richly bless you both and the community at Datron World Communications, Inc. It is a great company with an even greater mission and purpose in this world. The gratitude I feel toward both of you cannot adequately be expressed in words.

Thank you to Jeanne McGuire for creating most of the Table Talks at the end of each chapter. Jeanne, you have experienced the hypocrisy within the Church and yet your heart still seeks after the one true God. Your gift as a trainer and curriculum development specialist has profoundly touched so many lives. Your skills are fantastic, but your generous heart is even greater than your skills. Thank you, my friend.

Thank you to Kathy Sivba, my teammate and executive assistant at the Servant Leadership Institute. Along with your hard work in making this manuscript better, your skills as an editor and your experience as a writer have been invaluable. This book could not have been written without your encouraging words and your wonderful expertise. Thank you!

Thank you to my fellow pilgrims at The Way Christian Fellowship. Although our roots run deep in Anglican tradition and the sacramental life, you all have a kingdom perspective that moves beyond the various tribes within Christianity and seeks to live out fully what it means to be the People of God, the Body of Christ, and the Temple of the Holy Spirit. It is a joy to serve as your shepherd.

Thank you to all my many friends who have read parts of this book and have offered their comments and suggestions. The topic of the Church creates a visceral reaction for many, both sinners

Acknowledgments

and saints. Your comments have inspired me to keep my eyes on Jesus, the perfector of our faith. Thank you.

And most importantly, thank you to the Father, Son, and Holy Spirit. To God be the glory, great things he has done! Amen.

Preface

When I was a child, I would dress up as King Arthur. Bearing a plastic Excalibur sword and carrying a sparkling tin shield, I would pretend to slay dangerous dragons in my backyard. Hours would go by as I would slash and stab, jump away and glide to the side, avoiding the hateful heat of my enemy. Occasionally, I would get wounded. Falling to the ground, holding my ribs in great pain from the terrible tearing bite of the dragon, I would flay my sword toward the beast, directing my aim at his torso and finally plunging the double-edged dagger into the very heart of my adversary.

I was a hero. My kingdom was safe. At eight years of age, I had the power. All would bow down and acknowledge me as a commanding leader, heroic king, and omnipotent protector.

WHY DID I WRITE THIS BOOK?

As I got older, I put away the plastic sword and the tin shield but not the idea of power. Playing football in high school, I knew that it was the fastest and the strongest who received the most public praise and adoration. In college, several knee surgeries put an end to my future NFL Hall of Fame career. So I became a spectator of professional football while always still believing in the power of the sword and the shield. The move away from football propelled me toward the development of my spiritual life, eventually leading to seminary and graduate school.

What was fascinating to me was that most of the church leaders were also practitioners of the sword and the shield model of leadership. Leadership in the Church was defined in the same way as leadership in the world: size, skill, and speed. Whereas today's prime ideological conversation among theologians and clergy practitioners is the relationship of the Church to postmodernity, the chief topic in seminary then was church growth. Peter Wagner, Win Arn, and the esteemed church growth gurus at Fuller Theological Seminary had a wide audience in the evangelical world. They convinced future pastors about the importance of "homogeneity" and that "location, location, location" was as significant to the local church growth scene as it was to the real estate world. As an eager seminary student, I bought in 100 percent! Success meant size, and size meant souls. So I attended every conference I could afford and heard every church leader I admired so that I too could have the same success for my parish in reaching people for Jesus Christ.

Looking back now, I see that much of my theological education at three well-known evangelical seminaries on the American landscape and my graduate psychology education were inadvertently based upon leadership precepts of the sword and the shield. Yet when I used these symbols of leadership as a template in reading the pages of sacred scripture and in particular the life of Jesus Christ and his followers, I found the actual leadership strategies were based upon the *cross and the towel, not the sword and the shield.*

To be fair, there were some significant voices in seminary that spoke of the cross and the towel as a model for Christlike leadership. Unfortunately, what often was modeled by prominent preachers in chapel, demonstrated by lay and ordained leadership in churches, and written about by theologians uncomfortably conflicted with the servant leadership style of Jesus Christ. Jesus's style of leadership seemed liberating and life-giving. The Church's style of leadership seemed eerily similar to business or political models, with religious jargon added for positional leverage.

The truth is that I used to believe I was a second class Christian pastor. I didn't have a megachurch, a radio ministry, or even a book that millions would say had changed their lives. I felt God loved me because he had to—after all, it was on his business card. He died on the cross for me, but I thought he was much closer to other followers than he was to me. So I worked hard in trying to impress him in ministry. I thought it wouldn't hurt to try to impress some of his contemporary disciples as well, so they could say a good word to him about me. So I worked hard academically and ecclesiastically.

Before moving forward, I need to tell you another bias. I love the Church. You cannot study God's Word without realizing that the Church is significant to God. The Church is called the "Bride of Christ." In another place, the Church is described as the "Body of Christ." Both words would suggest that the Church's identity is found in Jesus Christ, and its intimacy is deeply enriched by its relationship to Jesus Christ. Whether it is a house church or a megachurch, an emerging church or a traditional church, a denominational church or an independent church, I love these communities that seek to live by faith, endure in hope, and walk in love to the glory of God.

I also love pastors. It doesn't matter to me whether they are priests or preachers, male or female, young or old; they are a special breed anointed by God to *shepherd God's flock* and *equip his saints for the work of ministry*. Several years ago, the noted author and scholar Dallas Willard told me in one of my discouraging times of ministry that the pastorate "is the greatest calling in life." I believe him! Pastors can influence more people, without limitation to age, status, or gender, to the kingdom of God than in any other calling. This book is dedicated to all pastors.

To God be the glory.

Introduction:
The Bubble Wrap Pastor

*"Today I quit being a Christian. I'm out. I remain committed
to Christ as always but not to being "Christian" or to being part
of Christianity. It's simply impossible for me to 'belong' to this
quarrelsome, hostile, disputatious, and deservedly infamous group."*
—ANNE RICE

Anne Rice writes metaphysical fictional thrillers for a living. In fact, she is quite good in her craft, and her vampire books have entertained millions of readers. As an atheist, she wrote books reflecting her world without God. But in 1998, Anne Rice returned to the Roman Catholic Church, made a profession of faith in Jesus Christ, and announced it publicly seven years later. In her first book on the life of Jesus, *Christ the Lord: Out of Egypt*, Anne spoke of an unusual phenomenon—a number of Jesus scholars actually "hated" the person they were studying.[1] Usually, scholars love the subject they are studying. I was impressed with her candor.

Reading her recent comments on her Facebook page, I was

again impressed with her candor and, at the same time, saddened by her experiences within the organized Church. You might say that she is only speaking of the Catholic Church. You might be right, but I don't think so. In her interview with *Christianity Today*, she states, "Christians have lost credibility in America as people who know how to love. They have become associated with hatred, persecution, attempting to abolish the separation of church and state, and trying to pressure people to vote certain ways in elections."[2]

Regardless of your position on Anne Rice or her recent decision, she addresses a very important point for all of us who seek to follow Jesus and care deeply for his Church—love. If what she is saying is true, she is saying that many of us have forgotten how to love. Jesus said that demonstrated love is the only apologetic, "Just as I have loved you, you also should love one another. By this everyone will know that you are my disciples, if you have love for one another" (John 13:34–35).

THE FALSE TEACHINGS ABOUT LOVE

We have been confused about the subject of love for a long time now. Some suggest that love is simply an emotional response—a feeling. Others will tell you that love is only an action. Some will indicate that love means to know the other. All of these definitions, by themselves, fall short.

Love is more than just feeling, acting, and knowing. Love can be experienced in *chronos* time—seconds, minutes, and hours—but the deeper, mysterious divine love is experienced in *kairos* time where it is an ever-present reality. You have experienced it when you have lost track of time while meeting with a dear friend, sharing a tender moment with your spouse or children, or watching a magnificent sunset at the beach. You have experienced this kind of love when the Spirit of God touches deep within your soul at church, whispering to you his guidance or comfort. In the meantime, the worship team is singing or the preacher is teaching, but you have lost contact with outside time and are living in the moment. This kind of love, *kairos* love, is when heaven touches earth. Or as Jesus teaches us in prayer for God's will to be done, "on earth as it is in heaven." The mystics call this experience *the contemplative life,* where love and life cannot be fully appreciated through activity, knowledge, or feeling, alone or combined. This kind of *kairos* love is a conscious willingness to fully enter life, just as it is, regardless of circumstances.

As church leaders, our capacity to experience and then share that kind of love has been diminished because we have been trained to live in the bubble wrap of professional pastoring.

THE BENEFITS OF A BUBBLE WRAP PASTOR

Can you imagine a magazine advertisement for that kind of pastor? The ad would probably read something like this:

The bubble wrap pastor is one of today's most popular ministry items. Bubble wrap pastors provide excellent protection for preaching to fragile, easily breakable people. And many in the congregation can find it fun popping the pastor's bubbles when they are done with him or her.

Bubble wrap pastors were an accidental discovery by two theologians, the Rev. Drs. Ima Wolf and U. R. Pro, in the early Constantine period that revolutionized the

Church. With nearly two thousand years of Christendom technology, the bubble wrap pastor has been perfected for your pleasure. The bubble wrap pastor can be received by your congregation in either modernistic polyethylene resin or the postmodern transparent plastic film, depending on your theology. The key feature of the bubble wrap pastor is the evenly distributed air cushions, in the form of air bubbles trapped between two films of clear plastic, to offer the pastor shock and vibration protection while serving as your shepherd.

Bubble wrap pastors vary in size and age, depending on the demographics of your faith community. They also are available as giant inflatable figures; the gargantuan inflatable bubble wrap creates a sense that your church is really important because of the television, radio, and media connectors installed in it. The giant-size pastor is guaranteed to increase retail traffic and allow for more active, year-round use of your facility.

This bubble wrap pastor is really more inexpensive than you would think and offers the congregation several distinct advantages. It offers good protection for both the pastor and the congregation, so everyone can avoid honest conversations about the difficult issues of life. Most of our bubble wrap pastors are lightweight theologically, so even the dullest seeker can easily understand the sermon. Environmentally friendly, politically correct, and biodegradable, the bubble wrap pastor will not touch any difficult issues that may polarize the congregation.

Bubble wrap pastors are readily available at theological seminaries, bible colleges, and, of course, other churches.

Introduction: The Bubble Wrap Pastor

They can be easily purchased on the Internet from church suppliers with technologically advanced websites. Consider buying them in bulk, so you can provide bubble wrap pastors in every ministry specialty, including children, youth, single, young families, recovery, and seniors. For those churches that do not believe women should be pastors, there are now bubble wrap directors available. They do everything a bubble wrap pastor does but without the title! So buy today and save, save, save!

I don't want to be a bubble wrap pastor. I am sure you don't either.

This book is about how to avoid being a bubble wrap pastor. It is designed to identify the roadblocks to liberating leadership in the contemporary church, provide inspiration to see God's vision for leadership in the church, and offer instruction on the key practices of Jesus Christ as a servant leader that we need to incarnate in our lives as pastors within our parish setting.

HOW THIS BOOK IS ORGANIZED

The Cross and the Towel: Leading to a Higher Calling is organized in three sections. Part I speaks of the leadership crisis within our churches with an emphasis on our struggles with the predicament of power. Over the centuries within the universal Church, we have adapted and assimilated to the lifestyle and leadership ways of the world concerning power. It has provided for church leaders and their followers an unprofitable, self-serving preoccupation toward status, size, and stability. As a result, the habitual deficiencies of church leadership for the most part have been thinking, speaking, and doing worthless things and justifying them in the name of God. I will provide not only an understanding of power in leadership, but also an outline of the three main imperfections that have distorted the gospel to the unbelieving world and distracted the church membership from fulfilling its God-given calling.

Part II focuses on the leadership challenge of leading with the cross and the towel. Whereas the first section speaks of our struggles with power, the second section provides the solution to the power issue. The solution, of course, is Jesus. We will focus on the critical metaphors related to his leadership style and the measurable impact Jesus had as a leader to others.

Part III zeroes in on the right kind of church leadership. For many church leaders this section will be the most beneficial because of the many practical applications. Each of the chapters will provide the essential characteristics needed for your ministry leadership to be in alignment with God's kingdom. Each characteristic is supported by scripture, is consistent with the traditions of the ancient church fathers, and has been spoken of by the mystic followers of Jesus throughout the centuries. These steps of transformation are needed if we are to overcome our self-serving need to acquire or protect power and to look good, feel good, be right, or be in control. Unfortunately, too many church leaders have tried to increase or protect their power using pretension, compliments, flattery, manipulation, or maneuvering. Those are not God's way. For the Church to be a witness "on earth as it is in heaven," church leaders have to stop creating seekers in their own image and start creating disciples in the image of Jesus.

Part I

THE LEADERSHIP CRISIS: LEADING WITH THE SWORD AND THE SHIELD

*"Almighty God, you have given us the grace at this time with
one accord to make our common supplication to you; and you have
promised through your well-beloved Son that when two or three
are gathered together in his Name you will be in the midst of them:
Fulfill now, O Lord, our desires and petitions as may be best for us;
granting us in this world knowledge of your truth,
and in the age to come. Amen."*

—St. John Chrysostom

John Chrysostom, considered one of the noblest Christian leaders who ever lived, was also a great preacher, priest, and later bishop in the Church. The world around him was crumbling. The Roman Empire was experiencing its very last breath as a world leader. The common people were more enamored with entertainment, particularly games filled with great violence. Along with his pastoral team at the cathedral, John Chrysostom fed the hungry, provided care for the orphans and widows, and taught the Word of God. Although a leader, John Chrysostom was a servant first. The people knew his heart and his deep passion for God. Thousands came to hear him speak. We are blessed because nearly twenty centuries later, we still have some of his sermons and his writings. In *The Glory of the Priesthood,* Chrysostom speaks of the two greatest dangers for church leadership: a desire for self-glory and leading for the praise of people.[1]

In the same way, Part I is a cautionary reminder to all of us in church leadership that we have a holy calling to inspire, equip, and encourage God's people for God's vision in a world that God deeply loves. Whether by adaptation of or assimilation to the world's way, the contemporary church leader has lost focus to lead with God toward a higher calling "on earth as it is in heaven" (Matt. 6:10 NIV).

1

Distorting Power

"The Powers are good.
The Powers are fallen.
The Powers must be redeemed."

—Walter Wink

The world is replete with symbols. Symbols represent the connections between individuals, communities, and cultures learning about profound mysteries of the divine and ultimate realities of humanity. The Greek word, *symballo*, means "to throw together, to connect." A national flag, for example, can be a symbol to connect the dots for a nation that believes in "liberty and justice for all." A blindfolded woman holding balanced scales for the courtroom is a similar symbol of justice blind to status, gender, or any other form of discrimination. A wedding ring is a symbol of a loving, exclusive covenant relationship between a man and a woman. A symbol, fully appreciated, has a way of informing the head while inspiring the heart.

The religious world is filled with symbols. In my Anglican world, every vestment, every candle, every color, and every furnishing is a symbol that provides a connection between mystery and reality. Whether we spend our time in the sacred or the secular or in international spaces or domestic, we live in a world of symbols.

A unique aspect of symbols is that we can only understand their meanings if we fully participate with others who place the same value on that symbol. For example, seeing the wedding rings on a married couple might indicate to you that they are legally married, but only those wearing the symbol can tell the depth, breadth, and height of the love between them. The national flag of the United States has greater symbolic meaning and evokes a greater visceral reaction for me than when I see the national flag of Brazil. I imagine the reverse would be true for Brazilian citizens seeing the American flag.

THE CROSS AND THE TOWEL

The two greatest symbols Jesus used to describe his ministry and the ministry he desired for his followers were the cross and the towel. These symbolic metaphors had different meanings throughout the centuries, but to the early followers of Christ, their meaning was power.

The cultural history of the cross is particularly distasteful. The cross was used as a painful form of execution, usually reserved for the worst offenders or those of the poorest rank in society. The cross was designed to inflict pain upon the recipient and create horror for the public. It was a vicious symbol of power.

In order to provide some order in volatile Palestine, the Roman leadership would flaunt their power with highly public executions upon the cross. The non-Jews viewed crucifixion as the worst

4

form of capital punishment, surpassing other horrible methods including being beheaded, eaten by wild animals, or burned alive. The Jews, based on Deuteronomy 21:23, viewed crucifixion as being cursed by God. There was no question that the Romans used the cross in acquiring and protecting their power over the Jews. The cross was a symbol of shame![1]

THE CROSS OF JESUS

The word *cross (stauros)* appears twenty-eight times in the New Testament. Add the word *crucify* to the number and the total in the New Testament adds up to eighty-two references. At no time in these passages did the authors of the gospels or epistles deny the shame and humiliation of the cross. However, the paradox is that the cross used by the Romans to take life is the very same instrument God used to give life. The ironic reality is that the symbol of shame became to the Christian the symbol of salvation. In essence, the hatred exhibited by mankind became love demonstrated by God.

Theologically, the cross is the means by which God accomplishes our salvation while simultaneously demonstrating Jesus Christ's sacrificial, self-giving, and saving love for humanity (Matt 26:28; Mark 10:45; 14:24; Rom. 3:25; Gal. 2:19–20; Eph. 5:2). The cross, for the follower of Jesus, becomes the ultimate icon of the fundamental way in living the Christian life.

THE TOWEL OF JESUS

Like the cross, the towel became a symbol of love through servanthood. To understand why, consider this: Feet get dirty.

They are especially dirty if your main method of transportation is walking. In antiquity, the Nike walking shoe hadn't been created, nor had the Ford Model T. All the common folk had for transportation were their sandal-covered feet. Most of the animals were used for packing luggage (supplies), and only the very powerful could afford chariot service. As a result, providing a way for travelers to wash their feet became an essential part of ancient hospitality. You can go as far back as Abraham to see the practice of washing the feet of travelers, feeding them, and allowing them time to rest (Gen. 18:1–8). Even the confused Lot, living in the soon-to-be condemned dwellings of Sodom and Gomorrah, offered hospitality to the two messengers by washing their feet and offering a place to stay (Gen 19:2). Most hosts, however, would not actually touch the feet themselves. They would provide slaves to wash the travelers' feet (1 Sam 25:41), or simply provide the water so the guests could wash themselves. Superiors, after all, were unwilling to wash the feet of inferiors.

That is why one of the most noteworthy testimonies to Jesus's servant leadership lifestyle appears in the thirteenth chapter of the Gospel of John. Jesus is meeting alone with his disciples just before his arrest and ensuing crucifixion. What we read in John 13 changes everything we normally believe about positional leadership, demonstrated power, and relationships (John 13:3–17). After a conversation with Peter about his reluctance to be washed by Jesus, Jesus demonstrates servant leadership through the towel: "So if I, your Lord and Teacher, have washed your feet, you also ought to wash one another's feet. For I have set you an example, that you also should do as I have done to you. Very truly, I tell you, servants are not greater than their master, nor are messengers greater than the one who sent them" (John 13:14–17).

You can certainly understand why Peter initially resisted. He felt unworthy and perhaps a little vulnerable. The sword and the shield, not the cross and the towel, formed Peter's idea of power. Peter witnessed the religious leaders using their power to lord over others in the same deft way as the Roman magistrate or imperial soldiers. Whether this power to dominate others was wielded by words or weapons, it certainly had the same effect on people. But Jesus showed Peter and the other disciples that their assumptions of leadership and power were wrong. Power, in God's design, was created for good. It was used to serve others.

One of the great temptations for church leaders is to be powerful. They often seek the prestigious position not because it is a calling of God, but due to a confusion of desires. But Jesus directed all of his followers to "take up your cross and follow me."[2] And after washing their feet, he taught his disciples to "do as I have done to you."[3] These symbols provide a more accurate measuring stick of leadership than a prestigious position.

WHAT'S THE DIFFERENCE?

The Gospel accounts of Jesus provide a different way of leading. Following his resurrection, his followers engaged in the same leadership patterns. Reading the ancient church fathers on leading and following, you will see displayed the same blueprint as Jesus and his first-century apostles. The leadership ways of Jesus and the ways of the world to influence others are strikingly dissimilar. The sword and the shield provide a distortion to God-given power. The cross and the towel endow us to fulfill our destiny as leaders.

7

The Sword and the Shield	**The Cross and the Towel**
Positional power	Personhood power
For the sake of self	For the sake of others
Followers follow out of fear	Followers follow out of love
End justifies the means	Means are important as the end
Insiders and outsiders	Love neighbor as yourself
Kingdoms of this world	Kingdom of God
Leaders who serve	Servants who lead
Entitlement	Humility

Both have power, purpose, and followers. But one will liberate life, and the other will limit life.

We have been created to live out the cross and the towel, but this is not an easy task, especially when the majority of the world is committed to leadership by the sword and the shield. The cross and the towel will provide to the world a gentle revolution of the present status quo of leadership. The cross and the towel will assist us in living "on earth as it is in heaven." The cross and the towel will transform us into better church leaders. The cross and the towel will allow the church to be the Church and not simply an institution of religious education and social reformation. The cross and the towel are what the world is asking for in the Church. The cross and the towel are the answer to their prayers.

In the next three chapters, we will outline the three primary reasons why the Church has adopted the ways of the sword and the shield in leadership. It will be an uncomfortable journey for us but a necessary one. Repentance, the willingness to change the way we think about our thinking, is the first step forward. It is my prayer that we will all receive this message in the manner it was intended: filled with love, grace, and mercy.

TABLE TALK

In this chapter, we observed the cross and the towel, the revolutionary service model of power that Jesus taught and practiced. We saw how even his disciples resisted his mission of service to others. The worldly concept of power, which uses the sword and the shield to control and protect power, can be a great temptation for church leaders. The following questions will help you to examine your attitudes about power and leadership in your own ministry. How do your own life experiences shape your current model of leadership? Ask yourself how closely your personal values and church practices align with Jesus's way.

1. What memories come to mind when you recall playing as a child? What leadership model do these activities represent? Who were your role models in this period?

2. In adolescence, to what activities and interests were you drawn? How did they bring you attention and praise? What leadership model do they represent? Who were your role models in this period?

3. As a young adult, what experiences influenced your choice to become a pastor? Who were your role models in this period?

4. Based on your life experiences, what model of leadership most influenced and shaped your thinking—the sword and the shield or the cross and the towel?

5. Describe which symbols of your church ministry are most important to you. Why are they personally meaningful?

6. What symbols are most prominently displayed in your church? How have you communicated their history, importance, and meaning to your congregants?

7. In what ways have you helped your congregants distinguish the key difference between symbols and acts of secular power and the power of servant leadership?

8. How could you engage your congregants to more fully understand the symbolic meaning and unifying messages of the cross and the towel? How would you help them translate those symbols into thought and action in their own lives?

9. In what specific ways can you educate congregants and encourage them to actively discuss the challenges of guiding themselves to act as servant leaders in a world that recognizes and rewards secular symbols of success and power?

2

Adopting Power Symbols

"Arrange it so that we will be awarded the highest places of honor in your glory—one of us at your right, the other at your left."

—MARK 10:37

The sword and the shield style of leadership may have ancient roots, but it still plays a significant role in our contemporary society. Just as war methods have changed in our tech-savvy world, the sword and shield style of leadership has morphed into pulpits, programs, and corner offices. However, this style of leadership is still all about acquiring and protecting power.

Unfortunately, the contemporary church in its various traditions has adopted three symbols within leadership that have left the Church impotent and unimportant to the world. Like the first-century Roman Empire, the Church today has models for leadership that make the senior pastor, priest, or bishop look more like a corporate leader than a man or woman of God.

There are many secular symbols of leadership in the world, but three symbols stand out in the contemporary church. Each symbol, when fully adopted, scars the reputation of the Church and its leaders and leaves behind many innocent victims. The first symbol adopted by the Church is positional power.

POSITIONAL POWER

One victim of positional power was John Christopher. John graduated from a prestigious theological institution that his father had attended two decades earlier. John loved the Lord and aspired to become a first-class pastor. His first assignment after seminary was in a conservative Presbyterian Church in Southern California. As an associate pastor, John felt this would be a good learning experience for him. The senior pastor's reputation within the denomination was excellent. Recently married, John was ready to learn, live, and laugh with his bride and his new church family.

The Church was known for its quality of services, innovative approaches to ministries, and growing congregation. A typical attendee on Sunday morning might not have noticed anything odd. But over time, John began to see abusive power on the inside.

John was on staff for several years before he was close enough to the senior pastor to experience the abuse of power himself. The senior pastor spent as much time acquiring and protecting power as he did preparing for his Sunday messages. He spread rumors about others, questioned people's motives, cut people off in midsentence, and displayed a sense of moral superiority as he talked to both the parish and his fellow clergy. Turnover was becoming significant among the staff. The senior pastor told his board that the departing staff were either unable to keep up with the pace of his growing ministry or uncooperative to the mission of the church. The church was growing, so the board accepted the words of their shepherd at face value. The pastoral staff, both those leaving and those remaining, were often silent, fearing their future prospects in church ministry could be damaged by a negative word from this well-known pastor.

John didn't know it then, but the overbearing behavior of his senior pastor was due more to a chemical imbalance than some sort of spiritual disease. Nevertheless, the senior pastor saw the actions of his staff as disloyal and became increasingly paranoid as they began uniting against him. It was clear that a battle for power was forming. The staff hoped that the board would support them instead of the senior pastor.

Soon the battle grew too large to be maintained within the walls of the church office. The congregation became aware of the issues, and they started to take sides. The situation began to affect church growth. Newcomers didn't stay long because they could feel the tension.

Finally, the church imploded. The staff left along with a significant amount of the congregation, and the senior pastor continued in the facility with the remaining parish members. In the newly founded church, John Christopher was designated the senior pastor. The members moved on in an attempt to heal and grow as a faith community. But the victims were scattered everywhere. Clergy, lay leaders, and church members who had expected that the new church was supposed to be different were wounded by the conflict. They all thought that if people believed in the same orthodox biblical truths, then everyone should behave in the right way. The frustration of the disillusioned church members could be summarized in the statement, "I mean, after all, we are all Christians, for God's sake!"

What happened? What happened was that the sword and the shield style of leadership had been applied at the church. Each staff member was trying to acquire more power or to protect their individual positional power over others. The sword and the shield mentality created a sense of entitlement among church leadership.

Entitlement breeds arrogance and lacks personal accountability. Entitlement moves people from childlike innocence—"It is not fair"—to a far more devilish perspective—"It is my right." Even if you are a "benevolent" dictator, entitlement blinds you to genuine compassion. Expressions of gratitude rarely leave your lips.

Now, please don't misunderstand. Every church, regardless of its traditional heritage, is structured around some model of positional power. Depending on the church governmental structure, positional power could be held by a bishop, an elder board, a senior pastor, or even a longtime pillar among the congregation. Positional power is often necessary to weave order from chaos, and it is extremely useful in providing the right resources to a potential need. However, positional power is still the lowest form of leadership. And if this kind of power remains unchecked, it becomes a source of evil to the pastor, people, and their parish.

PLEASURE PRINCIPLE

Along with positional power, the Church has adopted another symbol of leadership in the secular world: *the pleasure principle.* Churches and their leaders have become savvier in manipulating their power through emotional appeals, guilt-inducing letters, and empty promises.

Mary Hutchinson works for a direct mail and fundraising company for nonprofits, churches, and ministries. She writes:

Adopting Power Symbols

I got involved in Christian TV more than thirty years ago because of one thing: It had the ability to reach huge numbers of people with the gospel—people who never would set foot in a church. I was not really interested in changing the culture, or any political agenda, or being entertaining while promoting Christian morals. It was evangelism that caused me to dedicate my career to helping dozens of these broadcast ministries. Today, I feel betrayed by the industry. Let's call it what it is. With the billions we have raised, it is indeed an industry. Two months ago, I set out to test the responsiveness of a few dozen of these ministries. I selected small ones, giant ones, evangelicals and charismatics, across all the major Christian networks. Many I knew personally; some I have worked with and some I had never heard of before I began the test. But I was confident that if I asked any of them about the primary reason they were on television, they would say without hesitation: "To win the lost." I drafted a very simple letter under an assumed name. I thanked the ministry for being there and then asked how to accept Jesus into my heart. I enclosed a $20 bill and listed my address in a bit of an unconventional way.[1]

Here were the results:[2]

- 5 percent never responded at all

- 75 percent never addressed Mary's question about salvation

- 20 percent sent packages that contained a book and/or DVDs

- 80 percent failed to thank the new donor

After reading about Mary's experience, an executive producer of a large international ministry wrote back, "Many pastors are happy as long as their name and face are being expanded across the globe and measure success by the number of viewers, new names, new partners, overall income, full events, online product sales, and book deals."[3]

The pleasure principle has been adopted by Christian television and radio. Preachers seek more to entertain at the pulpit than to equip the saints for the work of the ministry. Churches seek to outdo one another in showmanship during services. New believers who are celebrities are interviewed at church. Products—the latest book, CD, or T-shirt—are hawked at the altar. Success in church is determined much as it is in a Fortune 100 company: What do the numbers say? How much revenue has been generated against expenses is as much a topic within the church board meeting as it is within a corporation. Attendance figures, special guest speakers, entertainment celebrities, and constant reminders to tithe are as much a part of the worship service as the reading of scripture or singing of worship songs.

Not too long ago, I was invited to a well-known church to hear several Christian comics tell jokes after a Saturday night service. They certainly made me laugh. I sobered up quickly when at the end of the entertaining evening, the senior pastor said to his congregation, "This is what church should be all about." I thought, *Really? Has the Church that belongs to Jesus Christ been reduced to mere entertainment? Have the people of God come to a church to be entertained, or are they here to be equipped in order to engage in the world?* I am sure the senior pastor didn't really mean his remark that way. He was probably just sharing that the Church should be marked with joy. Unfortunately, many do come to church to be entertained. And because of that, many of the people in the pews are learning to become a consumer instead of a disciple of Jesus.

PROFESSIONAL STATUS

The third secular symbol of leadership adopted by the church is professional status for the clergy. This is not to question the nobility of full-time parish ministry, or the importance of vocational credentials, or even the nature of the call of God upon our lives. However, we have turned the succession of the apostolic ministry, including the process of ordination, into a professional society filled with academic exams, psychological testing, and background checks. I know why we do it, and I am not suggesting we shouldn't do it. But passing the exams, getting the "okay" from psychologists, and avoiding significant crimes does not guarantee someone is called by God.

The Church, since its beginning, has ordained certain members for special Holy Orders by the invocation of the Holy Spirit and the laying of hands (1 Tim. 4:14; 2 Tim. 1:6). Their calling certainly will require appropriate preparation in scripture, spiritual disciplines, and social awareness of contemporary issues. Years may pass before the calling is fully recognized by the Body of Christ. After all, the call of God must be tested and confirmed. They are professionals only in the sense that they receive a salary from a church. But the contemporary church, like secular institutions, has developed a professional class within its leadership. How so?

Who Has the Largest Church?

Striving to move up the ladder in the ecclesiastical world is as common as trying to advance in the corporate world. Many of those in ordained ministry use their current churches as stepping stones to larger and more well-known parishes. Certain churches are aware of this syndrome and often look at their pastor as simply a professional chaplain to oversee their services and attend to the sick. The investment between parish and pastor becomes transactional instead of transformational. When one clergy addresses another in a social gathering and inquires, "How did your Sunday go?" they often mean, "What was your attendance?" Being the largest church in an area is a source of pride for clergy and often provides much recognition for accomplishments.

Who Has the Coolest Outfit?

Clothing is another focus of the professional leadership class. In my world, the purple shirt is equivalent to a three-piece Armani suit. It symbolizes the authority and power of a bishop. Before Constantine, many bishops wore green to symbolize new life. After Constantine, the bishops wore the royal color of purple to symbolize authority. The large pectoral cross, the miter, the bishop's ring, and the elaborately designed vestments remind us how far church leaders have come professionally from the days of the apostles.

If vestments are not your style, then you certainly can wear an academic robe and hoods at the pulpit to express your power and authority. Having three stripes on the sleeves of your robes, for example, indicates you are the recipient of a doctorate and provides a distinct message to others concerning your status.

In the laid-back evangelical world, pastors too have their own vestments. Sometimes it is a suit and tie, and sometimes, like in Southern California, it is Tommy Bahama slacks and open-collar shirt with matching shoes sans socks. Their accessories are a Bible in the right hand and a Starbucks Grande in the left. Business casual is the look of success for the contemporary pastor, and it is as much a vestment as the cincture, stole, and alb.

Who Has the Greatest Title?

Look at the ads in *Charisma Magazine* for future conferences, and you might be amazed at all the titles: Apostle; Doctor; The Reverend; Bishop, and so on. In my Anglican world, church leaders have titles that can often be longer than their names.[4] For example:

- The Archbishop of Canterbury is called "The Most Reverend and Right Honorable the Lord Archbishop of Canterbury."

- A bishop is called "The Right Reverend."

- A dean is called "The Very Reverend."

- An archdeacon is called "The Venerable."

- A canon is called, "The Reverend Canon"

- A clergy person with a doctorate is called "The Reverend Doctor."

- If you are a professor, canon, and Ph.D., you are appropriately addressed as "The Reverend Canon Professor John Smith, Ph.D."

The Orthodox churches (and other apostolic churches) address priests using the title "Father." Bishops, although viewed as equal in the Orthodox Church, have different duties and their titles can range from "Your Grace," to "Your Eminence," to "Your Beatitude."[5]

Catholics designate their deacons in written address as "Reverend Deacon Francis Carroll"; monsignors as the "Reverend Monsignor William Mulry"; bishops as "His Excellency, The Right Reverend William A. Smith, D.D. Bishop of Rochester"; their cardinals as "His Eminence, Thomas Cardinal Hand, Archbishop of Los Angeles"; and their pope as "The Sovereign Pontiff, His Holiness Benedict XVI."[6]

Depending on the denomination, Protestant titles can be fancy or rather bland. However, all the Protestant denominations seem to value the title of "Pastor" or use the designation "Doctor." Many conservative evangelical churches identify males as "pastors" but females as "directors" even though their vocational calling is similar.

THE JESUS WAY

The sword and the shield mentality has driven us to adopt the secular symbols of leadership: positional power, pleasure principles, and professional status. Yet it is those very symbols Jesus spoke against concerning the religious leaders in the Gospel of Matthew, "Everything they do is done for men to see" (Matt. 23:5 NIV).

The Jesus way for leaders avoids self-exaltation. "For whoever exalts himself will be humbled, and whoever humbles himself will be exalted" (Matt. 23:12 NIV). The Jesus way is servant leadership without vanity or self-serving ideas.

THE RESULTS OF ADOPTING THESE SYMBOLS OF POWER

Because the Church and its leaders have adopted the secular symbols of leadership to define success, believers within the Church have suffered. In psychological terms, they have suffered from "learned helplessness."[7] They lack the empowerment to become servant leaders engaged in the world as a witness to Jesus and become custodians who maintain the institutional church. If they have spent any length of time in the church, they have seen their pastors move from one program to another in an effort to grow the church. The result for them has been unhealthy physical exhaustion and spiritual deprivation, not healthy spiritual formation. Because leadership has adopted the secular models, five unholy characteristics have developed within most congregations:

- A fear of and lack of trust in leadership

- Apathy in contributing time, talent, and treasure to the church

- Confusion about God's mission for the world

- Disharmony within the local assembly as they strive for power

- Pew sitters and nonparticipants in God's kingdom

The Christian world wants the church and its leaders to be the Church of Christ, not a secular social institution with religious jargon. Unfortunately, the universal Church, the local churches, and the clergy have done more damage to their reputation as the Body of Christ because they have adopted the rule of the sword and the shield. It is not the way of God!

TABLE TALK

In this chapter, we looked at how church leaders have adopted the three symbols of worldly power: positional power, the pleasure principle, and professional status. We saw the way many church leaders compete to see who has the largest church, the best vestments, and the most impressive title. The results for congregations have been unhealthy. Church leaders need to practice Jesus's way and avoid self-exaltation. Take some time here to reflect on your experience with power.

1. In what ways have you experienced the abuse of positional power in the church?

2. Choosing one example, what behavior did you witness? How did this behavior affect others? How did you deal with the situation?

3. What ministries come to mind that seem primarily focused on showmanship and entertaining the congregation to build church size or revenue? To what extent have you been influenced by their apparent "success"?

4. In what ways did the achievement of professional credentials and other "rites of passage" enhance your self-esteem and confidence as a church leader?

5. How important are professional credentials in your evaluation of other church leaders? Do you believe that these credentials have enhanced their leadership effectiveness?

6. What leadership model most characterizes your church today? What practices are characteristic of the sword and the shield model of leadership? What practices are characteristic of the cross and the towel model of leadership? Give specific examples.

7. In your congregation, do the majority of congregants think and act as spiritually and psychologically empowered servant leaders, contributing their time and talents to the church's purpose? If not, what are your specific concerns?

3

Abusing Power

"But we will devote ourselves to prayer
and to the ministry of the word."

—Acts 6:4

Ted Haggard, the pastor of the fourteen thousand-member New Life Church and president of the thirty million-member National Association of Evangelicals representing forty-five thousand churches across the United States, confessed that he was engaged in a long-term sexual relationship with Mike Jones, a gay massage therapist. Once an advisor to President George W. Bush on religious issues and recognized by *TIME* magazine in 2005 as one of the most important evangelicals in the United States, Haggard had violated the trust of his wife, his children, his church, his colleagues, and his Lord.[1]

The shouts of hypocrisy boomed louder than the cries of disbelief at another Christian leader fallen. However, scandals are not reserved to Protestants. A few years earlier, the darkness within the Catholic Church had come to light when hundreds of sexual abuse cases had been reviewed after nearly always being hidden by the bishops to protect their priests. The Los Angeles Diocese alone agreed to pay more than five hundred alleged victims a total of $660 million in 2007.[2] The Los Angeles *Times* prepared a tally of the various settlements with the Roman Catholic Church in the United States:[3]

- Boston Archdiocese: $157 million paid to 983 claimants

- Portland Archdiocese: $129 million paid to 315 claimants

- Orange, California Diocese: $100 million paid to 90 claimants

- Covington, Kentucky Diocese: $85 million paid to 350 claimants

Whether it is pedophilia or infidelity within the clergy ranks, it is clear that the Church has been scarred by its leadership and, as a result, has suffered greatly in its witness to the world. But sexual impropriety doesn't even compare in numbers to the thousands of cases of spiritual abuse heard around the country. From mainline denominations to independent charismatics, from television preachers to parachurch organizations, power-hungry priests and pastors are spiritually misusing or abusing their congregants, participants, or viewers for their own personal gain. This abuse comes in various forms—theological dogmatism, rigid rules, coercive behavior, or guilt-inducing strategies—all designed to create a punitive parish atmosphere. Add some motives of self-promotion, unhealthy competition, or even unreasonable expectations, as well as a steady dose of bashing other faith communities, and you can barely tell the difference between these unchristian behaviors and a legitimate dangerous cult.[4]

But abuse is not just reserved to the clergy. Over the years as a pastor and a seminary professor, I have seen hundreds of cases involving the abuse *of* clergy by church boards or congregants—spreading rumors, constantly criticizing, holding secret meetings, or restricting their clergy's salary as a weapon. Those power moves can devastate the spiritual and psychological well-being of the pastor and his or her family.

THE EASY ANSWER

It's too easy to blame Ted Haggard, Catholic priests, or the hundreds of other persons involved with abuse. It's also too easy to categorize all faith institutions as hypocritical. The pre-existing conditions that led to this awful mess must be examined. Most people want to blame the person who lit the match in a gas-filled room. But why was there gas in the room in the first place? Certainly, the transgressors should bear responsibility for their sins or their crimes. But some conditions were present long before they lit their matches. What were these conditions?

IGNORING PRAYER AND THE WORD

If the first problem within church leadership is adopting the secular symbols of power in leadership (the sword and the shield), the second problem is more silent and yet as effective in destroying the vibrancy of the Church. In essence, we have reduced our spiritual integrity in church leadership by ignoring the Word of God and our prayers with God.

THE EARLY CHURCH

Several years ago, I was traveling through West Texas on my way to San Diego. The weather was typically hot for August, but because it was close to dusk, the oppressive heat didn't seem as bad as I entered the 7-Eleven for a Dr. Pepper. Next to the store was a storefront church with the sign that said, "The Church of the New Testament." I didn't want to be cynical, but I was tired from driving and a little cranky.

I wondered, *What New Testament church is it? Is it the one in Corinth with all the relationship problems, or is it the one in Laodicea that is spiritually lukewarm? After all, the early church had the good, bad, and the ugly.*

Or are they saying, "This church is dispensational in theology, holding a strict view of eschatology that is pretribulational and premillennial." Or is it the type of church government that they are making reference to in describing their church as a New Testament church?

I wondered aloud to no one in particular how we have complicated what Jesus and his apostles made simple. Let's look back to the first century, forty days after the Resurrection of Jesus Christ. From the Crucifixion to the time of the Ascension of Jesus, the apostles moved psychologically from despair to delight, helplessness to hopefulness, and fear to faith.

The Ascension of Jesus Christ transpired on the eastern slope of the Mount of Olives between Jerusalem and Bethany. This hill east of Jerusalem was the place where Jesus wept over the city's future destruction (Luke 19:30–44). Jesus spent the night in agonizing prayer at the Garden of Gethsemane situated on the lower eastern slope of the Mount of Olives (Matt. 26:30–42).

It was also at that same mount where Judas betrayed Jesus (John 18:1–3).

From the place of the Ascension to the Upper Room was less than a mile. It was most likely at the home of Mary, the mother of Mark (Acts 1:12; 12:12). Cyril of Jerusalem (CE 310–386), along with church tradition, identifies the modern-day site of Holy Zion Church located outside the Old City near the Zion Gate as the location of the Upper Room.[5] The Upper Room was filled with the eleven apostles; Mary, the mother of Jesus; the brothers of Jesus; and the several women who followed him in his earthly ministry. The scripture says, "They all joined together constantly in prayer" (Acts 1:14).

It is not the only description. Read Acts 2:42: "They devoted themselves to the apostles' teaching and to the fellowship, to the breaking of bread and *to prayer*" (italics added). After the release of Peter and John from prison, this new community following Jesus "raised their voices together in prayer to God" (Acts 4:24). The effect of their prayers was evident, because scripture states, "After they prayed, the place where they were meeting was shaken. And they were all filled with the Holy Spirit and spoke the word of God boldly" (Acts 4:31).

Their first business meeting in the early church involved prayer (Acts 1:24) as Matthias was chosen to replace Judas Iscariot as the twelfth apostle. Their second business meeting was the choosing of seven deacons to oversee the fair distribution of food to the widows. The Twelve, the current church leaders in Jerusalem, turned the responsibility over to the seven, prayed over the newly selected deacons, and then returned to their primary apostolic tasks of "prayer and the ministry of the word" (Acts 6:4–6).

Take a stroll through the Epistles of Paul and you see the heart of a servant leader in prayer. Paul writes to the church of Rome: "how constantly I remember you in my prayers at all times" (Rom. 1:9–10). To the faithful saints in Ephesus, Paul writes, "I have not stopped giving thanks for you, remembering you in my prayers" (Eph. 1:16). You hear the same message in his letter to the church at Philippi, "I thank my God every time I remember you. In all my prayers for all of you, I always pray with joy because of your partnership in the gospel from the first day until now, being confident of this, that he who began a good work in you will carry it on to completion until the day of Christ Jesus" (Phil. 1:3–6).

Congregational prayer and individual prayer were the very heart of the early church. If you read the book of Acts, you will see the constant examples of intercessory prayers for the saints and prayers of thanksgiving for God's gracious provision. Rather than spend time on structure, titles, and the name on their signs, they simply modeled Jesus and his priority in prayer.

WHAT WOULD JESUS DO?

Jesus spoke to his Father as naturally as a devoted son would speak to a loving dad. The prayers of Jesus were to him a source of spiritual strength that inspired, equipped, and encouraged him to continue his personal partnership with the Father on earth. Read the words of Jesus: "I tell you the truth, the Son can do nothing by himself; he can do only what he sees his Father doing, because whatever the Father does the Son also does" (John 5:19 NIV).

You'll find other examples in John 11:41 and John 12:49–50.

After Jesus fed the five thousand with five loaves of bread and two fish, the scripture states that "Jesus was praying in private and his disciples were with him" (Luke 9:18 NIV). Jesus thought prayer was so important for his followers that he taught them how to pray (Matt. 6:5–14). We get a glimpse of this special relationship between the Father and the Son in the high priestly prayer of Jesus when Jesus prays for himself, his disciples, and for all believers (John 17:20-26).

WHAT WOULD PASTORS DO?

Unlike Jesus, pastors will always pray as beginners. We know the basics of prayer: a conversation where we speak and we listen to our heavenly Father. But the endings in our prayers often betray our true intimacy. We close our prayers with "in Jesus' name" as if it is the spiritual equivalent of a magical formula to allow us into the heavenly gates. We misunderstand the words of our Lord when he says, "And I will do whatever you ask in my name, so that the Son may bring glory to the Father. You may ask me for anything in my name, and I will do it" (John 14:13–14 NIV). Yet we do not see that formula ending any of the prayers in the Bible.

"In my name" is a statement of relationship just like the Lord Jesus had with his heavenly Father. Like Jesus, who only spoke of what the Father told him and did only what the Father asked him to do, we as followers of Jesus must do the same with him. This intimacy, "in my name," is not one of entitlement but one of practical reality.

Unfortunately, our current scene within the local church has created barriers to genuine intimate conversations with our heavenly Father. Most pastors pray on the run, sometimes literally and sometimes figuratively. I have talked to several pastors who multitask with their prayers. Some run and pray, some swim and pray, some workout and pray, some listen to music and pray, some drive their car to church and pray, and some pray only when their job calls them to pray. They pray at the hospital over a sick parishioner, they pray with others at a board meeting, they pray before a congregational meal, and they pray when others are around and expect them to pray.

Because many pastors have adopted the secular symbols of leadership, they have become more chief executive officers than men and women of prayer. Their schedules are often so packed with appointments, events, meetings, and services that they have neglected what is most important as a shepherd and servant leader. If our schedules were a moral document of our prayer life, what would they say about our commitment to prayer?

IGNORING THE WORD OF GOD

In my office, I have two dozen books on preaching. Every book is designed to help me become a better communicator of God's Word. My homiletics professor told me in seminary that there are only two kinds of preachers: those who have an inflated view of themselves in their preaching skills and those who are completely delusional. (Personally, I think I switch back and forth.) Of course, I knew my professor was joking, but he was making a point about our integrity in relationship to the Word of God. It is not that we don't have great communicators at the pulpit because we do. Some pulpiteers can make us laugh and cry; they inspire and motivate their audience. Many of those preachers even do a great job explaining a passage of scripture as it was understood by the original readers.

So if we have so many good communicators, why are so few

congregants connecting to the power of God through the Holy Spirit? I believe it is because of conflicting intentions from the pastor and the congregation. On the one hand, most church leaders believe the Bible is God's inspired Word (2 Tim. 3:16–17). On the other hand, church leaders use the Bible as a springboard for sermon subjects. The scriptures become the tool they master for a sermon instead of a person being mastered by the scriptures for a life with God.

TALENT, CELEBRITY, AND TERRITORY

The clergy and the congregation have formed a silent agreement that has reduced the scriptural integrity in modern-day church leadership. Together, they have decided that competency is more important than character, communicators are more enjoyable than prophets, and sectarianism protects power better than kingdom thinking. We have reduced the scriptural integrity in leadership by becoming focused on talent, celebrity, and territory.

Talent

I love talented people. I admire their ability to do what many could never do. In sports, I admire the baseball athlete who can hit the ball farther, throw the pitch faster and with more accuracy, or run the bases faster. In dance, I admire the magical motion of the performers as they glide across the floor in rhythm. In music, I love the uniqueness of voice that moves you deeply to emotionally respond to the melody.

In the same way, talented pastors can be gifted orators, skillful counselors, artful administrators, and master motivators. They all deserve recognition for their contributions to the Body of Christ. However, we have become so oriented to talent that we forget that the main qualification of church leadership is character. Read the passages about leadership for the early church, and you will notice that character was more important than talent was.

- Seven men full of Spirit and wisdom were chosen to assist the twelve apostles (Acts 6:3).

- Bishops must be above reproach (1 Tim. 3:1–7).

- Deacons must be worthy of respect (1 Tim. 3:8–12).

- Overseers must be blameless and holy (Titus 1:6–9).

- Elders were asked to be examples to their flock (1 Peter 5:1–4).

The primary factor in the early church that distinguishes leadership from the world is character. It does not mean early church leaders are sinless. Look at the Apostle Paul's life before conversion or the Apostle Peter after conversion to see that truth (Acts 8:1–3; Gal. 2:11–14). Although imperfect, church leaders have a sustained track record that reflects godly characteristics.

Many churches, particularly the larger ones, have created a position called a teaching pastor. For the most part, the teaching pastor's role can be a wonderful idea for someone whose calling is to teach God's Word. However, more churches are calling teaching pastors who have no connection to their local community. Sometimes, the teaching pastor lives outside the community and flies in to teach on Sunday. Other times, the congregation watches a simulcast or video and never meets the teaching pastor in person. There is nothing wrong with having a teaching pastor on staff. But the teaching pastors and their families need to live in that faith community to provide ongoing credibility for their ministry.

Another talent that has developed into a revolving relationship for many churches is the worship leader. Again, the lack of accountability within the local church community has led many worship leaders to lead dual lives that are inconsistent with the message of our Savior.

Celebrity

There was a time when being famous meant being great—but not since the creation of television. There are people today who have gained recognition for having done little or nothing of significance. Celebrity status is purely a function of being well-known; consequently, publicity is the only qualification for fame today.

Throughout the last fifty years, some in the clergy ranks have attained social greatness and subsequent fame. Desmond Tutu, Martin Luther King, Jr., and Mother Teresa of Calcutta come to mind. Other clergy have reached the rarified air of true fame for their oversight of a movement, whether it is Pope Benedict, Archbishop Rowan Williams, Billy Graham, or Rick Warren.

Radio, television, and books have made some pastors into celebrities and some Christians into groupies. The Christian publishing industry often works in the same style as New York publishing houses. Celebrity Christian leaders mean substantial profits for the booksellers. Sadly, the average pastor feels inadequate as a minister of the gospel unless he or she has published a book, broadcast a sermon on the radio, taught at a seminary, or delivered a keynote at a conference. With Facebook, Twitter, LinkedIn, YouTube, websites, blogs, CDs, and books, pastors may develop an artificial image for their public that moves away from the more natural, slower pace of deserved recognition within a Christian community. Church conferences and major denominational events are full of attendees who want to be around well-known ministers in order to build their own recognition and power structure.

Contrast that attitude with the words of the Apostle Paul to the church at Corinth in 2 Corinthians 10: "The tools of our trade aren't for marketing or manipulation, but they are for demolishing that entire massively corrupt culture" (2 Cor. 10:4 *The Message*).

Or later in chapter 11, Paul writes about "those money-grubby 'preachers,' vaunting themselves as something special. They're a sorry bunch—pseudo-apostles, lying preachers, crooked workers—posing as Christ's agents but shame to the core" (2 Cor. 11:13–14 *The Message*).

Acquiring or protecting celebrity status is all about power. The temptation for it even came upon the Twelve just before they were nearing Jerusalem for the final time with the Messiah. The other ten lost their tempers because their fellow apostles, James and John, wanted greater positions of influence in God's kingdom. Jesus said, "You've observed how godless rulers throw their weight around and when people get a little power how quickly it goes to their heads. It's not going to be that way with you. Whoever wants to be great must become a servant. Whoever wants to be first among you must be your slave. That is what the Son of Man has done: He came to serve, not to be served—and then to give away his life in exchange for many who are held hostage" (Mark 10:45 *The Message*).

Territory

It is striking how many pastors look at other churches as competition. In my Anglican tradition, much like the Catholic tradition, parishes used to be responsible for a territory. All those that lived in that village, regardless of whether they attended church, were part of the parish. They were baptized as infants, married in the sanctuary, and buried on the church grounds. Usually there was only one church in a small village.

After the Reformation in 1517, the territories within Christendom were up for grabs. The Protestants were aggressive in preaching not only justification by faith alone, but also the evils associated with the Roman Catholic Church. Today, churches cross the boundaries that were once exclusively held by another faith group. For example, the Orthodox Church is upset that the Roman Catholic Church is in Greece, Turkey, or Russia. Originally, the church was simply the Church universal. According to the *World Christian Encyclopedia* published by Oxford University Press, Christianity today has 33,820 denominations worldwide![6]

As a result, an evangelical Protestant may see a Catholic priest in a collar and wonder if he knows Jesus Christ as his Savior. That same Catholic priest may wonder if that evangelical Protestant is really just a right-wing, independent, Bible-thumping fundamentalist who lacks any knowledge of church history.

Even churches in the same fold worry about their people going to another church. What will happen to our church financially?

What is wrong with our church youth program? Unfortunately in this fear-based model, the church focuses on maintenance instead of mission.

Territorial or protective churches become easily threatened and often convey a rigid and dogmatic view of the Church. Some of them are intolerant on minor points of Christian doctrine and view others with skepticism. Here are a few examples of power struggles that are more sectarian and less oriented toward the kingdom of God:

- Protestant versus Catholic

- Fundamentalism versus evangelicalism

- Males versus females in Holy Orders

- Infallibility versus inerrancy in Scripture

- Episcopal Church versus Anglican Communion

- Emerging church versus traditional church

- Left-wing versus right-wing political beliefs in the Church

- Progressives versus conservatives

The great fear for many traditional leaders, of course, is that one group will proselytize (read "steal sheep") from another group. However, the constant awareness of new life in the kingdom of Christ will render irrelevant fears of other faith communities intruding on your territory. Seeking and living in alignment with God's kingdom really makes competition between churches impossible. The crisis within the Church is not the lack of church members, but a crisis surrounding the right kind of leadership. Servant leaders, who seek to live for the glory of God, must give primary attention to prayer and the Word of God. The devastating result of ignoring these two means for godly leadership is a church environment that inoculates the congregant from genuine spiritual transformation.

THE RESULTS OF IGNORING SCRIPTURAL INTEGRITY IN LEADERSHIP

Because we have adopted the world's symbols of leadership and consequently reduced our scriptural integrity in power by ignoring prayer and the Word of God, those who attend church have become seeking consumers instead of disciples. As a result, the average follower within American Christianity has:

- A shallow theological understanding of the Cross

- Little commitment to genuine community

- A strong interest in the pursuit of "stuff"

- Serious struggles within his or her marriage or with his or her children

- Doubt of God's goodness in the midst of suffering

- Motivation that is politically driven instead of God-focused

- A life with little distinctive difference from the way non-Christians live

- Discomfort with prayer

If George Barna, David Kinnaman, and Gabe Lyons are right in all their research, the Church, its leaders, and its followers have a major image problem. They report, "In our national surveys we found the three most common perceptions of present-day Christianity are anti-homosexual (an image held by 91 percent of young outsiders), judgmental (87 percent), and hypocritical (85 percent)."[7]

Our leadership needs to change so our Church can be a better reflection of the light of the world, Jesus Christ. But there is one more problem associated with contemporary church leadership that needs to be addressed before we look at the solutions.

TABLE TALK

In this chapter, we reviewed the many abuses of power that occur within the modern church. We saw how church leaders can lose their way by ignoring such fundamentals as prayer and scripture. This spiritual neglect has resulted in churches that are preoccupied with such worldly concerns as talent, celebrity, and territory instead of focused on Jesus's message of service to others. Take a few moments to ask yourself the following questions about your own prayer life and your relationships with your church and your congregation.

1. How does your daily life reflect the importance of prayer?

2. When you pray, do you experience your prayers as a genuine and intimate conversation with God? Do you listen for answers?

3. In what ways have you taught your congregation to use prayer in their daily lives? Have you taught them how to pray? If not, how would you teach someone to pray?

4. How do you use scripture as the foundation of communication to your congregation? How have you empowered your congregants to use scripture in their own lives? What kind of improvements would you like to make?

5. When you hire a church staff member, what questions do you ask to determine his or her character? What questions do you ask to determine his or her church leadership model?

6. In what ways does your church staff "live in the community" that they seek to lead and teach? How could you improve their connection to and relationship with the community?

7. What power struggles do you see within your church? What are the causes of these struggles? What effect do these struggles have on your congregation?

8. What secular standards or power structures have you assimilated to or adopted? What tendencies would an outside observer see? To what extent are these tendencies also true of your congregants?

4

Confiscating the Power from Above

"But you will receive power when the Holy Spirit has come upon you, and you will be my witnesses."

—ACTS 1:8

At 4:15 PM, on August 14, 2003, a massive power outage occurred throughout parts of the Northeast and upper Midwest belts within the United States and in Ontario, Canada.[1] The blackout affected fifty-five million people. It covered eight U.S. states. The Canadians blamed the Americans for the power failure. And, of course, the Americans blamed the Canadians. The blame poured down from politicians to power plant operators to the failure of safeguard standards. Blame was everywhere, but what was the cause?

According to the United States–Canada Power System Outage Task Force, the origin of the shutdown was the failure of FirstEnergy Corporation to trim trees in Akron, Ohio! The overgrown trees placed a strain on the high-voltage power lines that snowballed into the blackout of more than one hundred power plants.[2] Cleveland, Detroit, Toronto, and New York City all went dark because of scruffy trees. A few neglected trees confiscated the power for millions of people. The billions of dollars invested in power plants were trumped by key leadership's lack of attention.

THE POWER OUTAGE IN THE CHURCH

We have a similar power outage within many parts of the Church. The blackout is not due to overgrown trees but to disbelieving Christian leaders on the power of the Holy Spirit. It is not that the leaders within orthodox Christianity deny the existence of the Holy Spirit or even the influence of the Holy Spirit; they simply are willing to settle for so little of the power in order to achieve their own personal agendas. Unfortunately for many in Christian leadership, ministry success is all about size, skill, and speed.

David E. Fitch, a professor at Northern Seminary and the senior pastor of the Life on the Vine Christian Church in Arlington Heights, Illinois, states in his book *The Great Giveaway* that we are forfeiting the ancient and apostolic practices that made the Church vibrant, healthy, and contagious. Fitch believes we in the Church have imported many ideas from the secular world, including our definitions of success, our styles of leadership, our methods of evangelism, our self-serving preaching, and our lack of moral education.[3]

Another pastor who agrees is Bill Hybels, the highly respected founding pastor of the megachurch Willow Creek Community Church. He was honest before God, his constituency, and his community when he stated several years ago that they had mostly failed in developing Christ-centered disciples.[4] Based on their findings, they have made a ministry shift from being seeker-driven to disciple-making in their programs. What they needed, Hybels believed, was for their church to become deeply entrenched as followers of Jesus.

The nondenominational Willow Creek Community Church is not the only church with this problem. In my Anglican world, the institutions we have developed through the centuries present barriers that have hindered personal incarnational formation through the Spirit of God. It is not that we should not have archbishops, bishops, priests, and deacons as servant leaders within the Church; it is that we have allowed the institution's spiritually insignificant outgrowth to be unchecked, like the trees in the Northeast Blackout of 2003. This has caused significant parts of the Anglican church to be a monument instead of a movement and to be more focused on maintenance than mission.

THE PREDICAMENT OF THE CHURCH AND ITS LEADERS

The Church is now defined as a building, a denomination, canons (church law), or even a location (Rome, Canterbury). This is contrary to what the ancient fathers of the Church taught us, that we are the Church because the Spirit of God indwells every follower of Jesus Christ, who is the head of the Church. Ignatius of Antioch, a bishop and student of the Apostle John, wrote, "Wherever Jesus Christ is, there is the Universal Church."[5] Iranaeus, a second-century bishop, wrote, "Wherever the Spirit of God is, there is the Church and all grace."[6] Even the present-day Holy Father in the Roman Catholic Church, Pope Benedict XVI, wrote, "The Church is constituted in the Spirit through the sacraments, above all through baptism and the Eucharist, and through the Word."[7] The Apostle Paul calls Christ, "the head of the body, the church" (Col. 1:18).

The Church can succeed in its purpose only if those outside it are able to identify what the Church's vision, mission, and purpose are in the world. The world must see what the Church embodies and transmits. Sadly, when the world is crying out for a church to be the Church, the Church wants to be like the world. The result is institutional thinkers who need money, prestige, promotions, power, control, titles, esteem, competition, and personal agendas. They use religious language to rationalize their self-serving agendas and justify their actions. For example, I have seen congregational governments vote their self-serving preferences and justify their actions as if directed by the Holy Spirit. Elders or vestry members vote on an issue without prayer and state the Holy Spirit has spoken. Clergy at conferences secretly meet in corridors or behind closed doors to secure their agendas, then publicly thank God, and tell everyone that the Holy Spirit has inspired the decisions.

THE PATHOLOGY OF THE CHURCH AND ITS LEADERS

Part of the problem is a personality disorder within the Church, which has been developing for some time. In the clinical world, a personality disorder is an enduring pattern of inner experience and behavior that is pervasive and inflexible and leads to relational and personal impairment in how someone may think, feel, see, react, and do. In the same way, a personality disorder exists within the institutional church that is also enduring, pervasive, inflexible, impulsive, and impaired. The problem is so enduring and pervasive that some are leaving the church in order to save their faith!

Confiscating the Power from Above

What are some of the characteristics of the personality disorder within parts of the institutional church and its leaders? Five characteristics seem to stand out: they are paranoid, narcissistic, dependent, borderline, and histrionic.

Paranoid

Paranoia is the pervasive distrust and suspiciousness of others. Parts of the Church have been quick to counterattack and react with anger to perceived insults. They are highly suspicious of society, other denominations, or parachurch groups; show an unwillingness to forgive others; and exhibit overt argumentativeness in discussing their faith. Read blogs by fundamentalist pundits, and you will see how quickly we condemn fellow Christians like Bono, Denzel Washington, or even evangelical leaders like Rick Warren or Billy Graham.[8]

In 2001, Reverend Pat Robertson blamed the September 11th terrorist attacks in New York City on "the pagans, and the abortionists, and the feminists, and the gays and the lesbians who are actively trying to make that an alternative lifestyle, the ACLU, People for the American Way—all of them who have tried to secularize America. I point the finger in your face and say, you helped this happen."[9] Recently, he explained the devastating earthquake in Haiti as a curse from Satan because of the Haitians' pact with the devil.[10]

Narcissistic

Narcissism is the preoccupation with success and admiration. Parts of the Church often have inflated their accomplishments. They exploit others to achieve their purposes, compare themselves favorably with famous people or organizations, and devalue the

47

credentials of those with whom they disagree. For example, the Church of England still reports inflated figures of active church membership instead of a more accurate church attendance. The presiding bishop of the Episcopal Church continues to report inaccurate information to the press about the number of churches and their members that have left the denomination over the last five years.

Dependent

Dependence is the excessive need to be taken care of and be reassured. In parts of the church, pastoral care is clinging behavior that includes excessive advice-giving and taking on unhealthy responsibility for the well-being of others. As a result, the parish feels incapable of functioning without a priest or senior pastor and requires constant attention. Some of those in the pew view the priest, deacon, or pastor simply as a professional chaplain whose primary responsibility is to pray for and call on them when they are sick.

Borderline

Borderline personalities have a pervasive pattern of instability in interpersonal relationships. Parts of the Church alternate between extremes of idealization and devaluation of their denominations, pastors, and churches. Because of their unstable self-image, the denomination self-destructs, the parish implodes, and pastors live in stress-related anger. Lives are damaged because of rage, rumors, and ungodly reactions of congregations and clergy.

Histrionic

Histrionic means excessive emotionality and attention-seeking. Parts of the Church have exaggerated expressions in sermons and blogs, are easily influenced by current fads, and spend an unusual amount of time trying to impress one another. Their preachers often make up stories to communicate biblical truth, and their churches become overly trusting of strong authority figures.

How did this personality disorder develop? Although many might disagree, I believe this transition was the result of erosion rather than an unexpected earthquake or volcanic eruption. The erosion took years, sometimes moving so slowly that church leaders rationalized that the erosion was the sovereign hand of God rather than the lukewarm heart of men. Three key elements caused this erosion: inattention to its primary mission, disconnection from its primary source of power, and disorder in leadership.

Inattention to Its Primary Mission

The mission for the Church is simply our committed participation in God's own mission to the world for the redemption of all of his creation. The resurrected Jesus engaged his disciples with an imperative to make disciples: "Go therefore and make disciples of all nations, baptizing them in the name of the Father and of the Son and of the Holy Spirit, teaching them to observe all that I have commanded you" (Matt. 28:18–20).

Because the living God makes himself known in Jesus Christ, it is imperative for the immediate eleven apostles and later the entire Church to make disciples (learners) to live and call others to live, according to teachings of Jesus throughout the world. The lack of attention to this primary mission of the Church has caused its members to look inward for purpose, creating places of fellowship designed simply for self-maintenance. In other words, this kind of lifestyle within the Church has created a lazy eye toward mission and a lukewarm assembly.

Disconnection from Its Primary Source of Power

Part of the reason for the Church's inattention to its primary mission is the disconnection from the power supply provided by God for the Church. The contemporary church has invested more dollars and time in secular techniques and methodology than it has in trusting in the power source of the Holy Spirit.

Luke's two volumes stress the connection between being a witness of Christ and the promise of the Father to provide power through the Holy Spirit for his Church. Just before the Ascension of Christ, Jesus says, "But you will receive power when the Holy Spirit has come upon you; and you will be my witnesses in Jerusalem, in all Judea and Samaria, and to the ends of the earth" (Acts 1:8 NIV).

Luke describes how Jesus appears to his disciples and says, "And see, I am sending upon you what my Father promised; so stay here in the city until you have been clothed with power from on high" (Luke 24:45–49).

Power and witness are clearly linked. The witness of God's chosen Messiah to the world can only achieve success when endued with power from above. However, the contemporary church often neglects to wait in prayer until it receives the power from God. These pastors want to get on with the work. They are fast-paced and task-oriented organizations, often driving their congregation to exhaustion and providing guilt through sermons on why we are not reaching the lost. For many within the Church, the Holy Spirit is the neglected third person of the Trinity. They react strongly against the charismatic and Pentecostal movements. When I was in seminary in Texas, for example, many of my cessationist professors accused John Wimber of the Vineyard movement and Peter Wagner of Fuller Seminary of devilish acts of magic and manipulation of people. These men (my professors were all men back then) loved the Lord but refused to move beyond their template of dispensational theology even to entertain the thought of healings, prophecies, deliverance, and tongues for the contemporary church.

Disorder in Leadership

Once a year during Holy Week on Maundy Thursday, my church practices foot washing. It is one of the most emotional times of the year for me. I observe teenagers washing the tired and often mangled feet of senior adults. I see the rich washing the feet of the poor. I am humbled when my feet are washed and deeply moved by the teaching of Jesus when I am washing the feet of another brother or sister in Christ. On my office desk is a statue of Jesus washing the feet of one of his disciples. Some days, I think the disciple is Peter. On other days, I picture myself in the disciple's spot. And one day, I thought it might be Judas. That thought had a profound impact on me to realize Our Lord knew his betrayer and yet tenderly, lovingly washed his feet.

There is a crisis of leadership within the Church. More explicitly, the crisis within the Church is the lack of *servant* leadership. Our calling in ministry as a witness to Christ is to live our lives as servant leaders. Church leadership today, in many circles, desires the power of the sword and the shield that comes from the secular world instead of the power of the cross and the towel that comes from Our Lord.

Is there a solution to all this in the Church today? I believe there is; and the next part will help us in leading ourselves and others to a higher calling within the Church.

TABLE TALK

In this chapter we saw how strong the pull of our human weakness is. Church leaders can become disconnected from God and fall prey to various psychological pathologies. These personality disorders within the Church can leave us fearful, prideful, or emotionally unbalanced in many other ways. When we distance ourselves from God's Holy Spirit, the vision, mission, and purpose of the Church is lost. The questions below will help you to assess how well your ministry achieves union with the Holy Spirit.

1. How would you define the primary mission for the Church?

2. What is the vision, purpose, and mission of your church? How does it reflect your understanding of God's mission? In what ways and how often do you communicate this to your staff and your congregation? How does it help you in conflict resolution and decision-making?

3. How would your congregants define your church's vision, mission, and purpose? In what ways do you encourage your congregants to have an individual mission and purpose that align with your church's mission and God's vision?

4. How do you experience the presence of the Holy Spirit in your life? To what extent do you rely on the Holy Sprit as an active guiding and empowering force in your life?

5. How do you help congregants understand the role of the Holy Spirit in their lives? What sources of inspiration and practices help them embrace the power of the Holy Spirit?

Part II

The Leadership Solution: Leading with the Cross and the Towel

"Almighty and ever-living God, in your tender love for the human race you sent your Son our Savior Jesus Christ to take upon him our nature, and to suffer death upon the cross, giving us the example of his great humility: Mercifully grant that we may walk in the way of his suffering, and also share in his resurrection; through Jesus Christ our Lord, who lives and reigns with you and the Holy Spirit, one God, forever and ever. Amen."

—BOOK OF COMMON PRAYER

The next three chapters are designed to provide solutions to the Church's current distortions of power. As we saw in Part I, these distortions are seen in how we, as church leaders, are adopting the traditional symbols of power, reducing the spiritual integrity of that power, and confiscating our only source of true power in the Holy Spirit. The solution to the distortion is, of course, Jesus. In chapter 5, you will observe the pattern of Jesus's leadership in public and private ministry. As the chief servant leader, Jesus inspired, equipped, and encouraged God's people toward God's vision in a world God deeply loves. In chapter 6, you will respond to the visible metaphors of Jesus's ministry that demonstrate his rule of life: love. The metaphors are the cross and the towel. Finally, chapter 7 will examine the success of Jesus's leadership. The measuring tool for all leaders is the transformational impact others have received by our lives. After all, there is "no success without successors."[1]

5

The Model of Jesus's Leadership: Moving from Success to Significance

"He who would have God as his Father must have the Church as his mother."

—CYPRIAN, BISHOP OF CARTHAGE

Where did we go wrong? When did we take the first detour from the directive and design by Jesus for the Church? Who was responsible? Some people in the theological progressive camp think Paul was responsible for creating a more hierarchical and hardened faith community. Others in the emergent camp think the responsibility for the detour belongs to Constantine, the emperor of Rome, who wanted one religion in order to unify his personal kingdom. Still others, like some of our Reformed friends, blame the medieval period, where power-hungry bishops within the western church moved away from the teachings of Jesus. Some even say Satan himself duped the Church and its leaders.

However, placing blame is less important than seeking a cure. We need to get back to a church, using the profound biblical metaphor, where Jesus Christ is the head and his disciples are his body.

The Church's chief purpose is not to help people have better marriages, raise better children, earn a better income, develop improved communication skills, or live healthier lives. The authentic church, by her very nature, is designed to keep all Christian and non-Christian institutions, along with their leaders, humble by reminding them that they are not primary.

GOD AS THE ULTIMATE

The Church must direct us to the Ultimate. The Ultimate is expressed well by the Prophet Isaiah when he says that we have been created for God's glory (Isa. 43:7). The Reformers, in their quest to know the chief end of humanity, state in their 1647 Westminster Catechism that the purpose of life is "to glorify God and to enjoy him forever."[1] You would have a difficult time disagreeing with either the prophet or the catechism, for both statements speak to the very heart of God.

The Church has been called to be a witness to the Ultimate, the Holy One. The same prophet just three verses later, in Isaiah 43, states, "You are my witnesses, says the Lord, and my servant whom I have chosen so that you may know and believe me and understand that I am he" (Isa. 43:10–11 NIV).

Being a witness is simply telling others what you have seen and heard in your encounter with the Holy One. Jesus was the perfect witness to the Ultimate. His heart on earth and the heavenly Father's heart were one heartbeat. Jesus's ministry was a divine love letter from the Ultimate about the Ultimate. It was indeed a revelation.

As the perfect witness to the Ultimate, Jesus spoke and did only what the Father would want him to speak and do.

Later, in that same passage, Jesus says, "I can of myself do nothing. As I hear I judge; and my judgment is righteous, because I do not seek my own will but the will of the Father who sent me" (John 5:30).

When Jesus predicts his departure on the cross, he says, "When you lift up the Son of Man, then you will know that I am he, and that I do nothing of myself; but as my Father taught me, I speak these things. And he who sent me is with me. The Father has not left me alone, for I always do those things that please him" (John 8:28–29).

Finally, in the section of the Gospel of John when Jesus speaks his last words to a public audience, he says, "For I have not spoken on my own authority; but the Father who sent me gave me a command, what I should say and what I should speak. And I know that his command is everlasting life. Therefore, whatever I speak, just as the Father has told me, so I speak" (John 12:49–50).

Jesus was a witness in thought, word, and deed to the Ultimate. Therefore, the Church, as the Body of Christ, is inseparable from the head, Jesus Christ. So, what does this mean to us in the twenty-first century as followers of Jesus?

First, we must be intentional in choosing relationship power over institutional power. Institutional power obligates you to preserve that organization and system structure. For the Church, it becomes more important to preserve your identity or religious affiliation than your obedience in following Christ. I have witnessed this reality firsthand in the Roman Catholic

Church and later in the Episcopal Church. Being "Catholic" or "Episcopalian" was a mark of membership into an exclusive club, where you might have heard about the owner of the club but never personally had a close relationship with him. My pastoral brothers and sisters have acknowledged the same dilemma within their own institutional structures.

It was not institutional power that Jesus spoke about for his community but a relationship power that transforms. Relationship power creates obligations to people, not to principles designed for institutional preservation and purposes.

We don't "go to" church; we *are* the Church, demonstrating the Father's love with Christ as our head and the Holy Spirit as the agent of transformation. We are defined by who we are in Christ, not by our powerful positions and specialized gifts within the institutional church. We gather as a people of God to worship, form an encouraging community, collectively pray, and utilize our spiritual gifts to exercise our relationship power with the world.

The institutional church, left to its own human devices, can only provide a power similar to the institutional powers of this world, where might equals right. The Crusades and the blood bath of the English Reformation can serve as two glaring examples of institutional power gone wild. On the other hand, the persecuted church in the first three centuries, powerless in the ways of the world, experienced the greatest power through social relationships. Humility, compassion, and noncoercion were the marks of the persecuted church. The result was a community that was committed to living their lives "on earth as it is in heaven." Their social power came through a deep love for God and for others (Matt. 22:37, 38; John 13:31–34). As the Apostle John writes in his late first-century letter to the churches, "If anyone has material possessions and sees his brother in need but has no pity on him, how can the love of God be in him? Dear children, let us not love with words or tongue but with actions and in truth" (1 John 3:17–18 NIV).

The great failure of both the religious right and the religious left is that they have the same institutional strategy in acquiring and protecting their power. Jesus would want nothing of their coercive tactics and manipulative influence over people.

Second, we must be imitators in how Jesus utilized relationship power. How did he utilize his earthly power on others? Was there a distinct pattern for us to observe about how Jesus related to people? Was that pattern utilized to develop his disciples for a lifetime of ministry? Absolutely!

THE JESUS WAY TO DEVELOP SERVANT LEADERS

The Roman army was probably the greatest single fighting force in world history. For nearly one thousand years, the Roman army maintained its fierce identity and provided consistent victories for the Emperor of Rome. The Roman army, by means of the sword and the shield, was trained to acquire and protect power. No one had a bigger sword or a stronger shield than the Romans.

Jesus chose a different way to influence others. In another ironic twist, Jesus used the cross as a symbol of victory and the towel as a sacrament of otherness. The cross and the towel demonstrated a love for others, and both metaphors can help us now to understand how we can change the world. The cross and the towel were the final symbols of Jesus's earthly ministry, but the pattern for this sacrificial love was seen in him from the very beginning. His entire rabbinic pattern, as Chief Servant Leader, was to develop leaders who would imitate their rabbi in life. They in turn would develop additional servant leaders, who in turn would develop other servant leaders. His teaching style was designed for transformation through the power of the Holy Spirit. The movement of that small simple band of his followers in the southeast corner of the Roman Empire became a flame that has engulfed the majority of the religious world today.[2]

HOW DID JESUS DO IT?

The easy answer is God did it. And it is true, no matter how much effort you make in doing something, if God chooses for it not to be successful—it won't be. However, if the pattern of church leadership is the cross and the towel, it would behoove us to understand and imitate his way for developing servant leaders. Jesus developed servant leaders by inspiring, equipping, and encouraging them for God's vision in a world God loves. Jesus's game plan had three significant parts:

1. Jesus inspired others by modeling God's kingdom.

2. Jesus equipped others by teaching about the source of connection to God's kingdom.

3. Jesus encouraged others by sending his followers to model and teach about God's kingdom.

The Jesus way of inspiring, equipping, and encouraging others to God's vision is seen more clearly in the synoptic gospels, the sequential historical accounts of Jesus's life, than in the more thematic Gospel of John. So we will use examples from Matthew, Mark, and Luke to examine Jesus's leadership.

MODELING

The Galilean setting surrounds the beginning of the public ministry of Jesus Christ. Jesus spent most of his life and ministry in the mountainous area in northern Palestine. The Roman administrative post in Galilee was the opulent city of Sepphoris, about three-and-one-half miles northwest from Jesus's hometown of Nazareth and about fifteen miles west of the Sea of Galilee. It is likely that both Joseph and Jesus, expert craftsmen and carpenters, worked on several of Herod Antipas's construction projects within Sepphoris.

Additionally, the fishing industry was robust in the Sea of Galilee. As many as 225 fishing boats set forth daily from the coastal communities. Many more people were casting their nets from the seashore. The agricultural industry was also thriving. Wheat, grapes, figs, and olives were exported along the key trade routes.[3]

As richly as the fishing and agriculture industries provided for the region, its greatest treasure was the educational system through the rabbis and the synagogues. Although it was separated from Jerusalem by Samaria, Galilee produced many of the leading and influential rabbis.

Clearly, the educational process was significant in first-century Galilee. At age five, boys were considered fit to study the first five books of the Old Testament in the *Beth Sefer* (elementary school). By the age of ten, they were ready to study the oral law. At thirteen, they had their *Bar Mitzvah.* At fifteen, the special students studied at the *Beth Midrash,* a secondary school, where they were taught by the resident rabbi of the community the "prophets and the writings," as well as the rabbinic interpretations. At age thirty, certain qualified males were able to become authoritative religious teachers.

Without question, Jesus was part of the educational system. It is also clear that Jesus, at the age of twelve, was a gifted student of the scriptures. The teachers at the Temple were amazed at his ability to understand and inquire about theological questions and religious issues (Luke 2:46–47). Luke sums up Jesus's educational, physical, and social development well: "And Jesus increased in wisdom and in stature and in favor with God and man" (Luke 2:52).

At thirty, Jesus began his public ministry with a central message that would create an interest to all faithful Jews: the kingdom of God.

Although Galilee lacked the modern-day conveniences of Twitter, Facebook, or even a telephone, word spread quickly about Jesus throughout several regions. Matthew provides us a clue of his growing popularity: "So his fame spread throughout all Syria, and they brought to him all the sick, those who were afflicted with various diseases and pain, demoniacs, epileptics, and paralytics, and he cured them. And great crowds followed him from Galilee, the Decapolis, Jerusalem, Judea, and from beyond the Jordan" (Matt. 4:23–25).

After the Sermon on the Mount, the crowds were "astounded at his teaching, for he taught them as one having authority, and not as the scribes" (Matt. 7:28–29).

Jesus Christ was modeling for his disciples and Galilean

followers the marks of the kingdom of God. A hopeless and helpless group of people, under the oppressive regime of the Roman Empire, was provided hope and help by this unusual rabbi now living in Capernaum. His communication style truly connected with the people giving all, including those who had no influence because of their status, a new way of living.

Jesus modeled the kingdom, and the crowd was inspired! As an exceptional rabbi, he chose his *talmidim* (disciples) (Matt. 4:19; Mark 1:17; Luke 5:1–11; John 1:35–51; 15:16). As was customary in that culture, they would leave everything to follow their rabbi. The learning times for his students were not the typical classroom hours we know today. Instead, learning took place seven days a week, twenty-four hours a day. They followed their teacher so closely that as he walked, they would have the dust of his sandals on their clothes. They listened, watched, and imitated their rabbi to become like him. They wanted to understand the scripture and how to put it into practice.

Jesus was training servant leaders for the kingdom of God. The followers had a limited view of God and themselves. Their worldview was colored by their oppressed status and the restrictive teachings of the religious leaders. To change a worldview, you need to inspire people to a new vision. That is exactly what Jesus did. Jesus talked about the kingdom of God, demonstrated the power of the kingdom of God, and moved them to a deeper and more profound understanding that their rabbi was more than a gifted teacher and healer. He moved them away from the concept that the Messiah would acquire his kingdom with the sword and the shield. No, the Messiah King would use a more clever strategy to change the world: the cross and the towel.

Jesus inspired his followers through modeling the vision of

the Kingdom; he also equipped them through his teachings. He was the cultural architect of a greater kingdom. Jesus modeled the kingdom of God through proclamation and demonstration. He preached in synagogues, ministered to the multitude, taught his disciples privately, talked publicly in parables, and demonstrated through miracles that he was, and still is, Lord over nature, demons, disease, and death. The hopelessness created by the oppression of the Roman Empire upon the Jewish people would gradually change. A gentle revolution was taking place near the Sea of Galilee, and Jesus was responsible. Jesus was breathing life into a group of people who had felt dead over their sins, hurts, wounds, and heartaches. Jesus was living in a world of broken hearts, and as the divine physician, he was providing healing. He inspired hope, but also as a *cultural architect* of the kingdom of God, empowered the people through his teachings.

Cultural architects are similar to professional architects in business. They produce a design for a structure that gives the building a form. The single most important concept in design is unity. A single message needs to be created within the facility itself and among the people themselves. They must have a clear starting point, ensuring that the individual elements will not dominate the overall design.

However, a professional architect is no lone wolf. In fact, architects would be entirely unsuccessful if they developed a design without understanding the client's needs, analyzing the surroundings, and observing the laws. They would also be unsuccessful if they did not have a team that would turn the vision into a reality. A cultural architect is the same. Abraham Lincoln could not have dealt successfully with slavery anymore than Martin Luther King, Jr. could have dealt with civil rights if they had not had a team of ordinary people willing to do the extraordinary to make the vision become reality. No one creates culture alone. People matter!

There was no greater cultural architect than Jesus Christ. He never entered a formal institution, but thousands of academic institutions around the world were established in his name. He never painted a portrait or sculpted, but artists created glorious images in cathedrals and city blocks in his name. He never had a license to practice medicine, but thousands of hospitals are committed to healing in his name. He never traveled outside the Middle East, yet children are being fed, houses are being built, peace is being restored, marriages are being saved, orphans are being adopted, and human trafficking is being dealt with all around the world in his name. With all the blemishes within the Church, the people of God are doing the work of God.

As a cultural architect, Jesus's single most important concept in his design was the "kingdom of God" (Luke 4:43; Acts 1:3). Clearly, Jesus had modest beginnings for this movement. If Jesus's beginnings were modest, his methods were even more counterintuitive to the power brokers of that day. Christ was not enamored with the positional power of Herod or the institutional power of Rome. His commitment was to a relational power that can only be ignited through the sacrificial cross and the servant's towel.

All three synoptic gospels reach the same climax in the first part of Jesus's ministry with a question to his followers: "Who do you say that I am?" (Matt. 16:13; Mark 8:27; Luke 9:20 NIV). Peter's response led Jesus to move to the second stage for developing servant leaders.

The Cross and the Towel

TEACHING

(Matt. 16:21–20:34; Mark 8:27–10:52;
Luke 9:18–19:27)

The Jesus way for developing servant leaders started with inspiration. Then he equipped the disciples through his teachings. Jesus strategically takes his disciples south to Jerusalem and spends more time with them instead of the crowds in order to teach them more deeply the truths concerning his mission in the kingdom of God (Matt. 16:21–20:34; Mark 9:2–10:52; Luke 9:51–19:10). This second stage was designed to equip them to serve in the kingdom of God. The first stage made it clear to the Twelve and the many followers that Jesus was indeed the Messiah. The second stage was designed to equip them to overcome their own preconceived, erroneous notions of power in God's economy. Whereas in the first stage Jesus demonstrated he is Lord over the spirits, humanity, and nature, the second stage was designed to show that the pattern of transformational leadership in this world could come not by the sword and shield, but through the cross and towel.

Jesus foretold his death and taught the apostles to still be his *talmidim*. In Matthew's words, "Then Jesus said to his disciples, 'If anyone would come after me, he must deny himself and take up his cross and follow me. For whoever wants to save his life will lose it, but whoever loses his life he will find it'" (Matt. 16:24–25 NIV). His message had three parts: denial of personal control of one's life, acceptance of the cross of Jesus daily in commitment even if it meant rejection or even death, and modeling the examples and teachings of Jesus faithfully.

The journey to Jerusalem provided Jesus many private times with his followers, particularly the Twelve. He teaches them during this time who is truly great in this world (Luke 9:46–48). He teaches them the cost of following Christ and changing the way they thought about God, others, and themselves (Luke 9:57–62). He not only inspired his followers to see the vision of God, he more fully teaches them how to be empowered to live out that vision.

SENDING

During his earthly ministry, Jesus inspired by demonstrating God's kingdom and equipped his followers by teaching them about God's kingdom. But the third phase of Jesus's ministry was very important in order to continue the work of the reconciliation of heaven and earth. Not only did Jesus inspire and equip God's people for God's vision in a world the Father deeply loves, but he also sent them off to proclaim and demonstrate the kingdom of God.

Jesus wanted his followers to shift their beliefs concerning the kingdom of God, the Messiah, the true nature of Israel, the value of people, genuine leadership, and servanthood, plus a host of other vital issues on life in relationship to God, others, and self. Jesus wanted them to move away from the sword and the shield mentality, which defined meaning in life as abundant strength, improved status, and great financial stability. His teachings and his practice were designed to liberate the rich and the poor, the saint and the sinner, the old and the young, the religious and nonreligious, and males and females.

The Cross and the Towel

In Luke 9, Jesus sends out the Twelve to proclaim and practice the kingdom of God (Luke 9:1). In Luke 10, Jesus sends out seventy–two additional disciples to accomplish God's kingdom-minded mission on earth (Luke 10:1). Jesus—as a great servant leader—inspired, equipped, and now encouraged his followers by sending them out to the world.

TABLE TALK

In this chapter we saw that the true purpose of the Church is to direct us to God, the Ultimate. We observed how Jesus used modeling, teaching, and sending as methods to develop his Church, train servant leaders who would live according to the cross and the towel, and inspire future generations to do the same. Take some time to evaluate how well you as a church leader are serving as a living example of Jesus's way.

1. In what ways do you seek to teach others to become *witnesses* of the Ultimate? How do you encourage them to describe what they themselves have seen, heard, and experienced in their own lives?

2. Do you actively encourage your congregants to tell their own stories of the power of the Holy Spirit in their lives and of their relationship with Jesus? What could you do to improve their sense of empowerment as disciples of Jesus?

3. How do you seek to model the behaviors of a servant leader?

4. How do you actively inspire and equip your staff and congregants to develop as servant leaders? What could you do to better inspire and engage the hearts and minds of your

people to act as servant leaders? What do you need to teach them?

5. In what ways are you creating disciples for God's kingdom? What is your education process? How do you teach people to communicate and build trusted relationships in a way that inspires and engages others? How do you know when they are ready to model and teach God's vision?

6. Based on your reading so far, what concepts have been most meaningful to you in redefining and revitalizing your power as a church leader?

6

The Measuring of Jesus's Leadership: Moving from Self to Saint

"As a good Christian should consider every place as holy because God is there, so he should look upon every part of his life as a matter of holiness because it is to be offered unto God."

—WILLIAM LAW

Our challenge as church leaders is to lead with the cross and the towel, not the sword and the shield. If we can do that on a consistent basis, then we have found the solution to the power problem. Our model has always been Jesus Christ. Through his servant leadership, Jesus inspired, equipped, and encouraged God's people to see God's vision for a world God deeply loves. Jesus moved his followers away from the traditional views of success. He wanted his followers to know what their lives could be if they lived in alignment with God's kingdom.

The kingdom of God works differently than the kingdoms of this world. To Jesus and later his followers, the recipients of the cross and the ones who wash one another with the towel receive the greatest power because their acts of love most closely align themselves with the heart of God. The cross and the towel were more than symbolic metaphors to Jesus. They were a call to loving service.

In light of the cross and the towel principles, how do you measure leadership performance? Does the size of your congregation, the square footage of your facility, or the status of your position indicate your leadership success, significance, or service? Those measuring tools have often left church leaders working to build institutions instead of incarnational disciples. They also create pastoral celebrities instead of Christ-centered servants. Finally, these measuring tools for leadership success provide church leaders and their congregation a territorial and competitive mindset toward other churches.

THE ONE THING

Church leaders need to find "the one thing." This phrase comes from *City Slickers,* the 1991 American comedy film, which touched every male struggling with middle age. In the story, Mitch, played by Billy Crystal, has just celebrated his thirty-ninth birthday. His two longtime friends are also struggling with midlife issues and are in danger of losing their families.

To reignite their lives, the three sign up for a two-week Southwestern cattle drive as cowboys. The cattle drive begins in Colorado with a grizzled old cowboy named Curly leading the team. Curly, played by Jack Palance, is tough and cantankerous and has little tolerance for these inexperienced cowboys. In the eyes of Mitch however, Curly is the wisest person he has ever met.

After spending the night searching and finding some stray cattle together, Curly tells Mitch the secret of life:

> *Curly: One thing. Just one thing. You stick to that and everything else doesn't mean s—t.*
>
> *Mitch: That's great, but what's the one thing?*
>
> *Curly: That's what you got to figure out.*[1]

And that is what every church leader needs to figure out. In studying the scriptures, I have found that the measuring tool for leadership in God's kingdom is just one thing: holiness. It may have other names like godliness, perfection, or sanctification, but it is still the one thing! The measuring tool for leadership is being like the greatest servant leader, Jesus Christ. In simple terms, leaders are measured by how much we act, think, and speak like Jesus would. This kind of leadership moves us from self-directed ministry, relying on our own skills and experiences, to a Savior-directed and manifested ministry. In other words, it is a movement from self to sainthood.

SAINTHOOD?

If the source of our unhappiness in life is sin, then it follows that the source of all our happiness is being fully united with God in all aspects of our lives. The scriptures make clear the high standard necessary in order to live a life of continual intimacy with our heavenly Father: "Be perfect, therefore, as your heavenly Father is perfect" (Matt. 5:48). Jesus's remarks clearly have Old Testament support (Lev. 11:44, 45; 19:2; Deut. 18:3).

The apparent impossibility of the task leads me to prefer Eugene Peterson's paraphrase in *The Message*: "In a word, what I'm saying is, Grow up. You're kingdom subjects. Now live like it. Live out your God-created identity. Live generously and graciously toward others, the way God lives toward you" (Matt. 5:48).

Perhaps the concept of perfection is why we struggle so much with the concept of sainthood. Our natural thinking is that sainthood is for the next life, not the current one we are living now! The Apostle Paul addresses the early Christians as "saints" in several of his letters (Rom. 1:7; 1 Cor. 1:2; 2 Cor. 2:1; Eph. 1:1; Phil. 1:1; Col. 1:2), but we as contemporary Christians squirm, twist, and even buckle to get away from the term. The Apostle Peter uses the word *holy* to express the same idea: "Be holy yourselves in all your conduct; for it is written, 'You shall be holy, for I am holy.'" (1 Peter 1:15).

Left to our own limited resources, there is no way that we can be perfect as our heavenly Father is perfect. Is there a solution to the dilemma presented to us? There is if we are willing to deal with the biblical passages honestly, look at ourselves authentically, and engage in the process of transformation.

FIVE FOUNDATIONAL CONCEPTS FOR UNION WITH GOD

We Can't Become Perfect on Our Own

"Being perfect as our heavenly Father is perfect" demands a union with God, which is unattainable through our own power. The rich young ruler account in Luke 18 bears witness to the impossibility of entering the kingdom of God by our own efforts (Luke 18:18-25). If we are honest about our initial thoughts as contemporary pastors, we would say that the rich young ruler is a perfect church member. He has means to give and seems inclined to help the church financially. He is young and obviously could attract more people his age to a graying congregation. He is a person of influence who has a successful track record in business. Plus, since his youth group days, he has been dedicated to the Word of God. In every observable way, he seems blessed by God!

Yet Jesus understands his idolatry. Although we do not know exactly what the particular issue of idolatry is, Jesus knows it involves his wealth. Jesus never hesitates to tell the rich young ruler what is needed for his salvation. The command by Jesus to forsake his riches seems to be designed solely for him. In contrast, Zacchaeus, the very wealthy chief tax collector, had earned his wealth by cheating others of their money. He demonstrates repentance and makes restitution for his past wicked ways, but he is not required to give away his fortune (Luke 19:1–10). However the rich young ruler, in contrast to Zacchaeus, has to give up his wealth in order to receive eternal life. So what is the problem?

Jesus says to those within earshot of the conversation, "Indeed, it is easier for a camel to go through the eye of a needle than for someone who is rich to enter the kingdom of God" (Luke 18:25). No wonder those who hear the comments of Jesus say, "Then who can be saved?" It is a good and honest question. We need to ask ourselves this question today. The first foundational concept of union with God is that we are powerless in our own efforts to achieve it. Jesus said, "Apart from me you can do nothing" (John 15:5 NIV). The Apostle Paul also confirms this truth in his letter to the church in Rome when he writes, "All have sinned and fall short of the glory of God" (Rom. 3:23 NIV). No one on their own power can achieve union with God.

We Can Become Perfect through the Power of God

"Being perfect as our heavenly Father is perfect" demands a union with God that is only attainable through the power of God. It sounds like a contradiction. What is impossible to attain is also possible to attain. Without God, our efforts are unsuccessful. With God, all things are possible. Mary, the mother of Jesus, questions the angel Gabriel's words about her impending pregnancy because she is a virgin. The angel replies, "For nothing will be impossible with God" (Luke 1:26–38). God is actually good at making the impossible possible!

The power of God, not our own efforts, secures that holy union. In the Apostle Paul's prayer for the church at Colossae, he writes of the necessity of God's power for believers to experience God's kingdom: "He has rescued us from the power of darkness and transferred us into the kingdom of his beloved Son, in whom we have redemption" (Col. 1:13–14).

When the Apostle Paul writes to the church of Corinth, he affirms our human inadequacies while acknowledging the true power: "But we have this treasure in clay jars, so that it may be made clear that this extraordinary power belongs to God and does not come from us" (2 Cor. 4:7).

Remember the patriarch Abraham and his beautiful wife, Sarah. They couldn't have children by their efforts alone. I love Paul's graphic description of him—"as good as dead." Eugene H. Peterson puts it this way:

> *We call Abraham "father" not because he got God's attention by living like a saint, but because God made something out of Abraham when he was a nobody. Isn't that what we've always*

read in Scripture, God saying to Abraham, "I set you up as father of many peoples"? Abraham was first named "father" and then became a father because he dared to trust God to do what only God could do: raise the dead to life, with a word make something out of nothing. When everything was hopeless, Abraham believed anyway, deciding to live not on the basis of what he saw he couldn't do but on what God said he would do.[2]

In the same way, Paul recognizes that without the power of Christ he would not be able to handle the many stressors placed upon his life. "In any and all circumstances I have learned the secret of being well-fed and of going hungry, of having plenty and of being in need. *I can do all things through him who strengthens me*" (Phil. 4:12–14, italics added).

Without Christ, Paul simply could not cope. With Christ, all things are possible. Jesus's own words in Matthew 5 must have startled the hearers of his sermon when he said of the current religious leaders: "For I tell you, unless your righteousness exceeds that of the scribes and Pharisees, you will never enter the kingdom of heaven" (Matt. 5:20). The scribes and the Pharisees were attempting to be perfect on their own terms. However, the religious leaders produced the wrong kind of fruit by their efforts: hypocrisy, competitiveness, and jealousy, along with a critical and judgmental spirit (Matt. 23).

Being perfect as God is perfect necessitates that our lives get submerged in God's life. Eternal life, kingdom living, and salvation all mean an ongoing active relationship with the King of Kings, the Lord of Lords, Jesus Christ. Jesus describes this kind of living in his high priestly prayer: "And this is eternal life, that they may know you, the only true God, and Jesus Christ whom you have sent" (John 17:3).

We Can Become Perfect through Consistent Intentionality

"Being perfect as our heavenly Father is perfect" demands consistent intentionality. Our power is not sufficient in achieving union with God. However, our power is indispensable to the development of that holy union. It takes effort to be holy. To achieve that union with God, we must dispose, order, arrange, and organize our lives so that we are able to *receive* that precious gift from God. As Dallas Willard puts it, "We are called to well-informed action in the process of our own spiritual growth."[3] The scriptures are replete with that truth. Here are just four examples:

From there you will seek the Lord your God, and you will find him if you search after him with all your heart and soul. (Deut. 4:29)

For surely I know the plans I have for you, says the Lord, plans for your welfare and not for harm, to give you a future with hope. Then when you call upon me and come and pray to me, I will hear you. When you search for me, you will find me; if you seek me with all your heart. (Jer. 29:11–13)

But strive first for the kingdom of God and his righteousness, and all these things will be given to you as well. (Matt. 6:33)

Indeed, to this very day whenever Moses is read, a veil lies over their minds; but when one turns to the Lord, the veil is removed. Now the Lord is the Spirit, and where the Spirit of the Lord is, there is freedom. And all of us, with unveiled faces, seeing the glory of the Lord as reflected in a mirror, are being transformed into the same image from one degree of glory to another; for this comes from the Lord, the Spirit. (2 Cor. 3:15–18)

None of these passages indicates that we earn union with God, but all of them inform us that union with God demands effort on our part.

As my friend Dr. Keith Matthews puts it, "the work of transformation is God's work in us, but we are not passive in the process."[4]

We Become Perfect through Personal Cost

"Being perfect as our heavenly Father is perfect" demands a considerable personal cost. Original sin and our ongoing personal sins create painful wounds for others and us. Many times the wounds create deep and severe psychological, relational, emotional, and spiritual problems. Much has to change in our lives in order to experience union with God. We need to rearrange, reorder, and repent of the ways we have thought, spoken, and lived. This is a necessary purification process. Although painful, it can provide great clarity and significant healing.

The gospels tell us to count the cost if we truly desire to have this union with God. Again, words from Jesus point to the considerable personal cost of experiencing God's kingdom:

Blessed are those who are persecuted for righteousness' sake, for theirs is the kingdom of heaven. Blessed are you when people revile you and persecute you and utter all kinds of evil against you falsely on my account. Rejoice and be glad, for your reward is great in heaven, for in the same way they persecuted the prophets who were before you. (Matt. 5:10–12)

Enter through the narrow gate; for the gate is wide and the road is easy that leads to destruction, and there are many who take it. For the gate is narrow and the road is hard that leads to life, and there are few who find it. (Matt. 7:13–14)

Whoever loves father or mother more than me is not worthy of me; and whoever loves son or daughter more than me is not worthy of me; and whoever does not take up the cross and follow me is not worthy of me. Those who find their life will lose it, and those who lose their life for my sake will find it. (Matt. 10:37–39)

Whoever does not carry the cross and follow me cannot be my disciple. For which of you, intending to build a tower, does not first sit down and estimate the cost, to see whether he has enough to complete it? (Luke 14:27–28)

The Apostle Paul and his colleague in the mission field, Barnabas, instructed the churches on how to enter the kingdom of God. It is not a pleasant thought to modern-day Christians: "It is through many persecutions that we must enter the kingdom of God" (Acts 14:22).

An unwillingness to pay the cost of union with God is probably why the Church often acts more like a social or secular institution. This unwillingness to pay the cost has also caused church leaders to use the power of the sword and the shield instead of the cross and the towel. This misapplication of personal power will almost always lead to personality-driven ministries and entertainment-driven worship services.

Perfection Is the Most Worthy Goal

"Being perfect as our heavenly Father is perfect" is both a worthy goal and infinitely worth it! There is nothing better than union with God! This union was the design and the desire of God from the very beginning. We see it in creation, and we read about it in the last pages of the Bible. From Genesis to Revelation, our union with God is the goal.

In Revelation 21, the Apostle John describes the new heaven and the new earth. In this passage, the author explains the relationship between the Church and Christ in the beautiful imagery of a holy marriage. The Apostle John then writes:

> *See, the home of God is among mortals. He will dwell with them; they will be his peoples, and God himself will be with them; he will wipe every tear from their eyes. Death will be no more; mourning and crying and pain will be no more, for the first things have passed away. (Rev. 21:3–4)*

The consummation of the kingdom of God is fully displayed in these verses. This passage marks the coming together of everything that is fully realized in God and his kingdom. Unfortunately, many believers are taught they cannot live this kind of life in the world today. They are taught that the kingdom of God does not happen until the Second Coming of Jesus Christ. Yet, Jesus teaches his followers to pray, "Your kingdom come, your will be done, on earth as it is in heaven" (Matt. 6:10). Since the arrival of Jesus in the first century, the inauguration of his kingdom allows the consummated future kingdom kind of life to intrude into our present life. We can live the life of the kingdom now. Paul explains it this way: "So if anyone is in Christ, there is a new creation: everything old has passed away; see, everything has become new" (2 Cor. 5:17).

This does not mean that the kingdom of darkness doesn't exist in this life, but it does mean that we can experience a new life filled with the marks of God's kingdom: righteousness, peace, and joy in the Holy Spirit (Rom. 14:27).

A deep, profound, intimate, transforming union with God is possible in this life!

But How Do We Get There?

The terrible secret among contemporary church leadership is that leaders are struggling with their spiritual walk as much as the average person on the street. All of us will often rationalize that our current state of spiritual discontent is about our busyness in life. Laity begins to believe that holiness is only possible for church leaders. It is simply not true. Bishops, priests, deacons, pastors, church staff, nuns, or monks do not have an exclusive claim to the "the secret sauce" in order to respond to God's call for union.

The problem is not our busyness per se or the kind of sauce we like. We struggle with our faith because of the sluggishness of our hearts. The measure of effective leadership within the kingdom, according to Jesus, is a movement away from standardized successes, ritualistic symbols, and selfish activity. It is also a movement toward significance, service, and sainthood.

The scriptures clearly reinforce the thinking of the mystics, the doctors of the church, and the apostolic fathers on the necessity of union with God. They seem also to be in agreement that there are three stages or phases to that transformation. Church leaders are not exempt from any of these phases. In fact, they must model and teach these phases to their congregation.

These three phases take time, in many cases a lifetime, and once a phase of transformation is complete, that doesn't mean that you will not need to return to it. All three phases can even be present within the multiple aspects of the individual's being. If the measurement of church leadership is holiness, then this process outlined cannot be an elective in a master of divinity program. In fact, if you are a seminary student reading this book, this has to be a requirement for graduation in God's academy of lifelong learning. All the other classes are simply electives to help you get there.

THE FIRST PHASE: THE WAY OF CLEANSING

Mystics call this phase a necessary progress toward perfection. It often consists of conscious moral purification through spiritual disciplines, subjugation of distracting desires, and austere practices. The way of cleansing is designed to open our eyes to unrealized idolatry and initiate intimacy with our heavenly Father. It is a movement away from self and a movement toward living your life for the sake of others.

Abraham had to go through this phase when God tested him with the command to sacrifice Isaac, his precious son (Gen. 22:1–12). Moses, along with the Israelites, witnessed the way of cleansing in their forty-year wilderness sojourn on the way to the Promised Land (Deut. 8:2–3).

Peter experienced the way of cleansing many times in following Jesus as an apprentice apostle. His three denials of Jesus during the trial were painful, but they were clearly used by God as a way of cleansing. The moving account of Peter's betrayal in the gospel shows not only how God can redeem the darkness of the world, but also how God can utilize these terrible experiences for our growth toward union (John 18:25–27; 21:15–19).

The initial days of conversion for the Apostle Paul in Acts 9 was the beginning of his way of cleansing, purging himself of his pharisaical thinking about the Torah, followers of the Way, holy living, and God. No doubt the three years in the Arabian desert postconversion were a continuing process for Paul to unlearn many of the old ways of living and learn the ways of God (Gal. 1:13–20).

We really should not be surprised about the first stage. Every apprenticeship requires unlearning old things and learning new things. It is true in making furniture, playing sports, or living life in union with God. This phase is the first of several training processes for those who are disciples of Jesus. It is designed to bring your life into conformity with the ways of God and the spiritual practices necessary to maintain that relationship. This phase is mandatory for the leader who desires to serve God's Church.

However, it is in the way of cleansing where we are most likely to give up the spiritual journey because this phase can often be the most difficult.

What Needs to Be Cleansed?

The list is almost as different as the people on the journey toward union with God. However, here is a list worth considering. People need to be cleansed who:

- Are serving two or more masters

- Have lukewarm hearts

- Are careless about sin

- Have affection for sin

- Try to be self-reliant

- Ignore the God moments in life

- Deny God's love, power, and goodness

- Have an incorrect image of God

- Have deep habits of sinning

- Are intellectual snobs

- Experience emotional instability

You can probably think of some other areas, but you get the drift. The prodigal son provides a superb illustration of the way of cleansing. The prodigal son, known as the younger son in Luke 15, had all the characteristics named above plus a fondness for travel and debauchery (Luke 15:11–31). The prodigal, while living in a foreign country, squandered his reserves. He had to look for a job. The prodigal didn't accept the position at the pig farm because he thought that it was a good career move. No one else would hire him. This pig farm was the place of last resort! The New Revised Standard Version states the prodigal "came to himself" (Luke 15:17). In other words, he finally came to his senses.

The way of cleansing is a process of coming to our senses. Cleansing starts a process of seeing reality accurately—God, the world systems, others, and ourselves. Cleansing begins our journey toward union with God. In this first phase, we actually begin to think and act differently. We even begin to feel differently, and our desires begin to change. As we move closer to the ways of God and the "mind of Christ," we begin to take on his characteristics and patterns of love.

THE SECOND PHASE: THE WAY OF LIGHT

The mystics call this stage the illuminative way. Ralph Martin, an assistant professor of theology at Sacred Heart Major Seminary in the Archdiocese of Detroit, describes this experience in his book *The Fulfillment of All Desire*:

> *The illuminative stage is one of continuing growth. It is characterized by deeper prayer, growth in the virtues, deepening love of neighbor, greater moral stability, more complete surrender to the lordship of Christ, greater detachment from all that is not God, and increasing desire for full union.*[5]

The Measuring of Jesus's Leadership: Moving from Self to Saint

In modern-day language, we have moved from dating God to actually being engaged to God. Using the biblical example of Luke 15, we have moved from being the prodigal son to experiencing God as the elder son. We have made an important transition in how we live our lives. In the first phase, we moved from living for the sake of self to living for the sake of others. In the second phase, we moved from living for the sake of others to living for the sake of God.

The elder son in Luke 15 experienced great stability in his relationship with the loving father. However, it is clear in the account that the elder son knew his father but did not have the heart of the father. He lacked an awareness of his own condition or lacked a desire to be like his father.

The elder son is like many of us in Christian ministry. Our church leadership is consumed with ministry. After many years as caring pastors, we have moved from living for ourselves to living for the sake of our faith community. We have sacrificed financial gain to serve for the sake of others. We have worked long hours for the sake of others, and we have received unfair criticism from those we have served.

Henri Nouwen wrote a spiritually stunning book entitled, *The Return of the Prodigal Son*. The motivation for the book was his chance encounter with a reproduction of Rembrandt's painting of the subject. As time went on, Nouwen saw himself more as the elder son:

Ever since my friend Bart remarked that I may be much more like the elder brother than the younger, I have observed this "man on the right" with more attentiveness and have seen many new and hard things. The way in which the elder son has been painted by Rembrandt shows him to be very much like his father. Both are bearded and wear large red cloaks over their shoulders. These externals suggest that he and his father have much in common, and this commonality is underlined by the light on the elder son, which connects his face in a very direct way with the luminous face of his father.

But what a painful difference between the two! The father bends over his returning son. The elder son stands stiffly erect, a posture accentuated by the long staff reaching from his hand to the floor. The father's mantle is wide and welcoming; the son's hangs flat over his body. The father's hands are spread out and touch the homecomer in a gesture of blessing; the son's are clasped together and held close to his chest. There is light on both faces, but the light from the father's face flows through his whole body—especially his hands—and engulfs the younger son in a great halo of luminous warmth; whereas the light on the face of the elder son is cold and constricted. His figure remains in the dark, and his clasped hands remain in the shadows.⁶

The elder son lives nearer to the father than the prodigal, but he is still lost. When the younger son arrives home, the elder son is filled with resentment for the many sacrifices he has made for the sake of others and for the sake of his father.

Church leaders, including me, try to do the right things, obey the laws, and seek to be hard working. Generally, church leaders are respected for their kindness, generosity, and moral standards. Church leaders, including me, also seem unusually gifted in building resentment; condemning others even if they are from their own flock; and with self-righteousness, lashing out at the uncommitted.

It is in the second phase where we develop the Christian virtues of faith, hope, and love. It is in the second phase where we learn to separate our successes as pastors from our true significance in Christ. It is at the end of this second phase where we experience genuine liberty from possessions, money, sensuality, fame, pride, impatience, anger, and other lustful disorders. We actually begin to learn humility from all the experiences of humiliation. This process helps to heal our need to defend our reputation, look good to outsiders, or be in control. Our soul's capacity increases in direct proportion to the amount of love we are able to receive from God.

THE THIRD PHASE: THE WAY OF UNION

As a zealous Pharisee, Paul was steeped in the tradition of the Torah. He relied completely on his own power to achieve godliness. His self-reliance and his colossal efforts at holiness failed. It was a form of godliness but lacked the genuine power of God behind it. But when Paul met Jesus on the road to Damascus, all changed. You can read about Paul's phases in Acts, Galatians, and the two letters to the Corinthian church. His unitive experience is clearly stated in several verses in the Book of Galatians:

I have been crucified with Christ; and it is no longer I who live, but it is Christ who lives in me. (Gal. 2:20)

And those who belong to Christ Jesus have crucified the flesh with its passions and desires. (Gal. 5:24 esv)

The Cross and the Towel

But far be it from me to boast except in the cross of our Lord Jesus Christ, by which the world has been crucified to me, and I to the world. (Gal. 6:14 ESV)

Paul had experienced the one heartbeat with God. He had experienced what Our Lord Jesus prayed to the Father for all of his followers, "I in them and you in me, that they may become perfectly one, so that the world may know that you sent me and loved them even as you loved me" (John 17:23 ESV).

The final phase, the way of union, is knowing and loving as we are known and loved by God. Each phase toward union with God gradually but steadily increases our capacity to love God, one another, and ourselves as God loves. The greatest commandment found in the Gospel of Matthew now becomes a reality for those who live as Jesus lived: "You shall love the Lord your God with all your heart, and with all your soul, and with all your mind" (Matt. 22:37–38).

Let's review the important transitions in how we live our lives so that we can become genuine stewards, caring shepherds, and passionate teachers.

THE WAY TOWARD UNION WITH GOD

If the first phase was dating and the second phase an engagement, the third phase is a spiritual marriage. The third phase is the perfect union of wills, and every action is ruled by love. The church leader now has the empowerment to follow all the commandments of God and the callings of the Holy Spirit. After all, Jesus lives in us and through us. Fear has been eliminated because perfect love casts out fear. The third phase is where you can genuinely experience a love for your enemies and also great fruitfulness in your prayers. The unitive phase is always a place of growth characterized by greater conformity and participation in the love of God through the crucified life. Your life sufferings have a new meaning. During the first phase, you questioned God about your sufferings. In the second phase, you are willing to suffer for God. In the final phase, you take on the suffering of Christ. Your heart moves from rebellion to repentance to redemption.

Living like the Father is the third way. It is filled with generosity, love, forgiveness, tenderness, and truth. The third way still lives in the kingdoms of this world, which are filled with darkness, but is simply unmoved by the temptations it offers and deeply moved by the God he or she loves. The third phase, the way of unity, is the fulfillment of all desire. It becomes a holy dance between a King and his bride.

WHAT ARE THE MEANS OF GRACE TO GO THROUGH THESE PHASES?

As we follow Jesus, we are formed by him. Part III will address the practical ways we can reach this stage as church leaders. However, be mindful of the means God uses in this transformative process. In fact, the means of God's grace are the same in every phase. The triune God (Father, Son, and Holy Spirit) in action is a means of grace. The Word of God is a means of grace. The universal Church, manifested in the various communities of God, is a means of grace. The holy sacraments are a means of grace. Participating in the liturgy, reciting the creeds, and having conversations with God are means of grace. Individuals, institutions, and circumstances outside of church life are often used as means of grace.

God is not silent, nor is he apathetic about our desire to be in union with him. God is interested primarily that we begin to think, feel, and act differently. The means of grace are designed to give us a heavenly worldview. That is why both John the Baptist's and Our Lord Jesus's very first imperative to those seeking the kingdom of God was to "repent."

In those days John the Baptist came preaching in the wilderness of Judea, "Repent, for the kingdom of heaven is at hand." (Matt. 3:1–2 ESV)

From that time Jesus began to preach, saying, "Repent, for the kingdom of heaven is at hand." (Matt. 4:17)

Unfortunately when we think of repentance, we think of some crazed judgmental fundamentalist holding a billboard with the word, "Repent!" emblazoned on it. I didn't think these billboard carriers really existed anymore until I was entering Staples Center in Los Angeles, California, for a Lakers basketball game. I was shocked to see that not only do they exist, but there also are many of them. But that is not what John the Baptist or Jesus had in mind when they used this important word.

The word *repent* is a combination of two Greek words in the New Testament that mean to simply "change one's mind." Dallas Willard states that it is a call to "think about your thinking."[7] This change of mind on how you think about God and the kingdom will certainly provide a change in the direction of how you live your life. If there is eternal life—and there is; if there is a kingdom of God—and there is; if there is a heaven—and there is; if there is a Savior to the world—and there is, then all of our lives must be evaluated in the light of these foundational truths. We need to have that heavenly worldview in order to have the correct perspective on life and on our leadership style.

In the third and last section, we will see how God uses that heavenly perspective in helping us become better servant leaders in our local congregations.

TABLE TALK

In this chapter we learned that holiness is the one true calling for church leaders. Our goal is sainthood for ourselves and our congregations. We should not let this calling overwhelm us. Scripture tells us that nothing is impossible with God and that perfection is attainable through his grace. Grace is available in abundance throughout our work of transformation, from cleansing, to light, and finally to union with God. Take a moment to reflect upon both your progress and your challenges in your personal journey toward God.

1. How do you measure your own performance as a leader and pastor?

2. To what extent and in what ways do you seek to act, think, and speak like Jesus? What are two examples that come to mind? Would you describe these acts as "holy"?

3. How would you help others move through a process of personal transformation to an intimate union with God in this life?

4. In what ways has your own life reflected the three phases of movement toward unity with God? Tell at least one personal story that has occurred in each stage.

Part III

The Leadership Creed

"O God, you have taught us to keep all your commandments by loving you and our neighbor: Grant us the grace of your Holy Spirit, that we may be devoted to you with our whole heart, and united to one another with pure affection; through Jesus Christ our Lord, who lives and reigns with you and the Holy Spirit, one God, forever and ever. Amen."

—Book of Common Prayer

Creeds are words we live by as a community. Creeds have been developed in times of war in order to inspire a nation to never give up, and creeds have been created in times of peace to inspire people desiring to live for a mission. The word *creed* comes from the Latin *credimus* ("we believe") or the singular *credo* ("I believe").

The best creeds are communal loyalty oaths. The early church had a three-word creed that defined them as a people, "Jesus is Lord." The creed spoke of their loyalty to One and only One. That Christian creed made it clear to the Roman Empire that Caesar was not lord and to the Jewish population that Jesus was the Messiah. Those three creedal words of the early church honored the great creed found in the *Shema Israel* of Deuteronomy, "Hear, O Israel, the Lord our God is one Lord. And you shall love the Lord your God with all your heart and all your soul and all your might," and clarified to everyone whose kingdom these followers would serve (Deut. 6:4).

The more developed ancient church creeds like the Apostles Creed and Nicene Creed simply amplified the earlier compressed expression of belief for the early church and explained more fully the Christian understanding of the *Shema Israel.*

This last section, in three chapters, is our leadership creed as servant leaders. These chapters will help us to understand that we have been given two resources from God. In order to fully utilize these resources, all church leaders need to make three significant vows in their vocation. Because of the resources provided and our willingness to live out these vows, we can now strategically and tactically lead ourselves, and others, to God's higher calling.

7

Prayer and Scripture: Two Gifts for Every Church Leader

"The Christian leader of the future is the one who truly knows the heart of God as it has become flesh, 'a heart of flesh,' in Jesus."
—Henri Nouwen

Securing the way of unity as a consistent way of living is impossible by our own efforts but certainly plausible when empowered by "the Lord, the giver of life."[1] Striving toward that unity with God demands a revelatory self-knowledge and knowledge of God. Unless we are willing to engage extensively with the two primary gifts God provides, our insights will remain fruitless, assessments will be inaccurate, and our decisions within the church will be misapplied. The two gifts for all church leaders seeking that unitive experience with our heavenly Father are prayer and scripture. Both gifts are designed by God to provide an ongoing conversation between divinity and humanity. Granted, God provides the same gifts to all, but church leaders seem to be especially called to receive these gifts because of the unique priorities of their ministry within the world.

The two gifts are God's tools of revelation to us. He reveals himself through these means of grace. They are not the only means God uses, but they are his primary means for touching the soul of humanity. Jesus tells us, "My sheep hear my voice, I know them, and they follow me" (John 10:27). The voice of Jesus is heard most clearly during our times in prayer and in the Word of God.

CONTEMPLATIVE PRAYER

Henri Nouwen, a Catholic priest, psychologist, professor, and author, wrote a small masterful book entitled, *In the Name of Jesus: Reflections on Christian Leadership.*[2] Nouwen writes of the deep longing for modern-day clergy to be relevant and how most attempts by clergy to become relevant in the world have been met with resistance in the secular society. Nouwen believes the resistance has let a "deep current of despair" exist among clergy.[3] As a remedy to the despair, Nouwen encourages all clergy to have a different perspective. In fact, he believes the clergy can be more effective in this world by not imitating the world's relevant experts but, in his own words, to become "irrelevant."[4]

Jesus risked irrelevance in his day by simply offering himself to others. Despite a lack of society's credentials, lives were deeply touched by his vulnerable love. The spiritual discipline necessary in developing that mindset, according to Nouwen, is contemplative prayer. He writes, "Through contemplative prayer we can keep ourselves from being pulled from one urgent issue to another and from becoming strangers to our own heart and God's heart."[5]

Contemplative prayer is a conversation, spoken or silent, between your heavenly Father and you. Bill Hybels, the founding pastor at Willow Creek Community Church, refers to it as hearing God's whispers.[6]

All of us want our prayer life to become more connected and more impactful. Our error often comes when we look at prayer as a technique instead of a relationship. When Jesus was teaching his disciples about prayer, he showed them a relationship with their heavenly Father is possible (Matt. 6:5–15). If we simply see this as a technique for prayer, we have missed the entire point of his guidance. Prayer is designed to cultivate a wonderful relationship. Building that kind of relationship with God, like all important relationships in life, takes quality time, focused attention, and loving nurture.

Paying attention to God is the heart of all prayers. Prayers can be uttered hurriedly (Luke 23:42); privately (Acts 10:2, 30); publicly (1 Cor. 14:14–17); secretly (Matt. 6:6), or in a group setting (Matt. 18:20). Prayer breathes life into our hearts. As Therese of Lisieux explains, "For me, prayer is an aspiration of the heart, it is simply a glance directed to heaven, it is a cry of gratitude and love in the midst of trial as well as joy; finally, it is something great, supernatural, which expands my soul and unites me to Jesus."[7]

It is insignificant to God whether our prayers are spontaneous or written, memorized or read, mental or vocal, or voiced in song or in prose. What counts in prayer to the Almighty is the attentive recognition that we are speaking and listening to God. Although we are all, to some degree, apprentices in effective contemplative prayer, I have found the following suggestions to be helpful in my own life:

- While in a relaxed position, quiet your body and mind into a peaceful state, remembering to breathe easily. Imagine the peace of God flowing through you. The psalmist writes, "Be still before the Lord and wait," and, "Be still, and know that I am God" (Ps. 37:7; Ps. 46:10). Be gentle with yourself, but let go of all the things that are causing stress, anxiety, and worry.

- Because the Lord is near, draw yourself into his presence (Matt. 28:20; Phil. 4:5; Isa. 49:15). Francis de Sales writes, "Begin all your prayers, whether mental or vocal, in the presence of God."[8] Imagine yourself entering his kingdom and coming into his presence.

- As you enter his kingdom, keep your thoughts fixed on Jesus, the express image of God (Heb. 1:1–4). See him before you as the resurrected and glorified Christ (Rev. 1:5; 21:1–8). If you have trouble focusing, choose one event in his life to meditate on. Perhaps a scripture verse comes to your mind. Say the passage quietly or feel free to read the passage. Picture yourself in the biblical passage. See yourself as a disciple learning at the feet of Jesus.

- As you are coming into his presence, now see our Lord Jesus being present *in* you (Col. 1:27). Respond to his presence by giving thanks. As you become more accustomed to praying this way, you will experience a peace and joy that is overwhelming because you are in his light (John 8:12; 12:36; Rev. 22:5).

- Because prayer is about relationship, dwell on his love for you and your love for him. Scriptures may flood your mind. Perhaps other thoughts (his whispers), will catch you. There might be a sin to confess or some action you must do. You might simply be in profound awe with the Almighty as tears run down your cheeks. It is all okay. Turn your mind upon yourself, seeing the Lord touch areas of your body or your thoughts that need healing. God might also bring to your mind the appointments you have scheduled today or this week. Ask the Lord to sanctify the tasks in his holy love. Listen and yield to his promptings. Do not rush; you are with the King (Col. 3:3).

- Once you have prayed for yourself, ask God to provide you the names of those who need intercession. In the state of prayer, relax and allow the Spirit of God to speak to you about his children who need your intercession. Although prayer lists can be helpful, this type of praying isn't about lists as much as it is about listening to your Father's voice about those in need (Col. 1:9; James 5:16).

- Express gratitude for his holy light and fantastic love. As you are ending your prayers, offer yourself as a living sacrifice this day before him (Rom. 12:1–2). Be sure to renew your protection, armed with his power in the Holy Spirit (Eph. 3:14–18; 5:10–20). Give thanks that you are filled with the fullness of God (Eph. 3:19).

These are only suggestions for making prayer more meaningful in your life. Be sure to make space for the Holy Spirit's loving work as you are in holy conversation. Prayer is that wonderful connection between his Spirit and ours, his love and ours, and his healing perfections upon our imperfections.

One of the most exciting parts of my day is having a conversation with my wife; how much more so must it be to have a conversation with the living God who knows you and loves you more than anyone else on earth or in the heavens. Contemplative prayer is really a deep sharing between two very close friends.

SPOKEN PRAYERS

As an Anglican, I have recited prayers directly from the scriptures and from our prayer book. Often these prayers are beautifully succinct, yet they have profound meaning for all followers who desire to grow in prayer. Additionally, many of the ancient church teachers have also encouraged the followers of Christ to pursue daily the rhythm of prayer found in the "Divine Office." These liturgical prayers set by appointed hours throughout the day have become a vital part of public and private worship in Catholic, Orthodox, and Anglican churches around the world. The early church was the genesis of these types of prayers. The early Christians, nearly all Jews, continued the Jewish practice of reciting prayers at designated hours throughout the day (Acts 3:1; 10:3, 9). The three times of prayer in the Second Temple Period for Judaism were 9 AM, 3 PM, and sunset.[9] The spoken prayers of the early church community included reciting or chanting of Psalms. Designated passages in the Old Testament were also read. Later, the sacred writings of the gospels, Acts, and epistles were added to the Old Testament readings. The early church was devoted to the activity of prayer (Acts 2:42).

HOW SHOULD YOU START?

Some excellent prayer books can help you in this journey. Eugene Peterson's book, *Answering God: The Psalms as Tools for Prayer*, can serve as a primer in teaching you how to pray the Psalms. Leanne Payne's *Listening Prayer: Learning to Hear God's Voice and Keep a Prayer Journal* is particularly helpful. The *Book of Common Prayer* or the *Celtic Daily Prayer* will provide you rich times in prayer, with designated hours of focus throughout the day and night. For my practice, the sections in the *Book of Common Prayer* on morning prayer, noon-day prayers, evening prayers, and compline are wonderfully supportive in my spiritual walk. All of these prayer books can be used individually or in community.

Is there anything wrong with spontaneous prayers? Absolutely not! However, the ancient leaders of our faith saw the tremendous value associated with using contemplative and liturgical prayers in their spiritual development. These types of prayers provide a genuine stilling of the soul. In our fast-paced society filled with distractions, we need the "stilling of our soul" even more than the ancients did. By the way, during your prayers, don't be afraid to use soft music, light a candle, or apply other mood settings that might help you enter the present moment with your Lord.

How much time should you spend in prayer? It is a good question. As a young seminary student, I lived in guilt that I didn't devote the same hours to prayer as the great reformer Martin Luther did. People said that he spent three hours a day in prayer before he even started his busy schedule. I don't even know if that is historically accurate, but it worked well on my guilt. I especially felt guilty when the first thing I wanted to do in the morning was get a cup of coffee from Starbucks. My guilt increased when I read Paul's directive to "pray always for this is God's will for you" (1 Thess. 5:16–18).

If you, too, experience guilt, remember the purpose of prayer. The purpose of prayer is to develop a relationship with God. A deep relationship is intensified when you begin to know God and love God as we are known and loved by God. Your prayer life is a demonstration of your desire for unity. Followers of Christ modeled this with a constant state of prayerfulness, where they recognized his presence at all times, mentally listening and sharing with the Almighty. However, you cannot pray at all times effectively if you do not set aside specific times for prayer.

If we are to lead ourselves and others to a higher calling, prayer is one of the two greatest gifts God gives us as leaders. This is especially true for those leaders who want to live out the precepts of the cross and the towel and avoid the traps of the sword and the shield.

SCRIPTURE

Leading ourselves and others to a higher calling demands that we receive another gift of God's grace: his Holy Word. In receiving, understanding, and sharing God's revelation, the apostles were keenly aware of the importance of prayer and scripture (Acts 1:14; 6:2). During a congregational conflict surrounding the distribution of food for the needy, the apostles spoke clearly about their priorities:

Prayer and Scripture: Two Gifts for Every Church Leader

Therefore, brothers, pick out from among you seven men of good repute, full of the Spirit and of wisdom, whom we will appoint to this duty. But we will devote ourselves to prayer and to the ministry of the word. (Acts 6:3–4).

The first-century Jews and the early Christians treated the writings of Moses and the prophets as the very oracles of God (Luke 16:29–31). To both the Jew and the Christian, the words of God were infallible. The words were open to interpretation, but no one questioned the source of the illumination (Deut. 18:15–22).

Although Jesus's own interpretation of the scriptures was clearly different than the religious leaders of that day, he treated the law, prophets, and writings as completely authoritative and divinely inspired (Matt. 5–7; Luke 4:14–30; 24:13–49). The Apostle Paul also viewed the Old Testament scriptures as divinely inspired, "All Scripture is breathed out by God and profitable for teaching, for reproof, for correction, and for training in righteousness, that the man of God may be competent, equipped for every good work" (2 Tim. 3:16–17). The only scripture for the early church was the Old Testament. The early church interpreted the scriptures in the light of Jesus Christ.

During the later apostolic times and early patristic times, the New Testament was also viewed as divinely authorized by God (2 Peter 1:12–21, Didache, 1 Thess. 1:2–10; 4:1–8; 5:19–20).

The scriptures are filled with both powerful prose and poetry that lead us to the way of union with God in heart and mind. This experience, having one heartbeat with God, demands an interactive, continuous, and intentional humble relationship with scriptures. Eugene Peterson, in *Eat This Book,* writes, "Christians feed on Scripture. Holy Scripture nurtures the holy community as food nurtures the human body. Christians don't simply learn or study or use Scripture; we assimilate it, take it into our lives in such a way that it gets metabolized into acts of love."[10]

God wants for his children an incarnational theology that works in everyday life. Leading ourselves and others to a higher calling demands that we no longer use the Bible for sermon preparation alone, as a weapon against cults and nonbelievers, or as an endorsement of our political opinions.

As a church leader, you need to understand the various Bible battles concerning infallibility, inerrancy, views of authority, historical criticism, and propositional truth. However, you must move beyond the Bible battles so you can lead your flock to a higher calling from God.

HOW SHOULD YOU READ?

Here are some suggestions on reading the scriptures for spiritual transformation:

Expect God to Be There

Treat the Bible in your hands as something holy. Don't toss it on your desk or pick it up again without the realization that the pages before you are sacred. In these pages, God is revealing himself to us. We do not worship the Bible, but we do worship the God of the Bible. God is the central character in all the stories—after all, it is his story. The written Word also informs us that Jesus Christ is the living Word. Expect the living, ever-present, all-knowing, completely loving, always truthful triune God—the

Father, Son, and Holy Spirit—to be present with you when you open *the Book*.

Allow the Scriptures to Tell the Story

A life story may be told in a thousand photos but never just one. If this is true about us, it is even more so with God. His revelation about himself unfolds through the pages of the scriptures, culminating in his fullest visible expression in Jesus Christ. Allow the scriptures to tell the story of God. God is the central character in all the books in the Bible. As you read, see how God desires to engage in the lives of those in different times and different settings.

Release the Need to Be in Control

King David, in the Bible's longest Psalm, writes, "Your word is a lamp to my feet and a light to my path" (Ps. 119:105). Without that lamp that illumines his light, our way in this world can be pretty confusing. Our willfulness (our desire to be right, feel right, look good, and be in control), can stand in the way of objective perceptions about ourselves, others, and God. Often, our wounds in life reinforce this willfulness. We can become fearful, agitated, anxious, and angry if we sense that we are alone in our struggles. Our personal kingdoms usually don't work very well. God desires for us to be willing, not willful, to experience his kingdom. To let go of our limited power, we need repentance and the ability to change how we think. Because life is a series of entering unknown territories, following unclear directions, battling through impossible odds, and dwelling on unfulfilled promises, God desires us to trust him at his word.

Identify with the Characters and the Events in the Story

Early in my life, I strongly identified with David's risky passion and zeal before he was king. In my late thirties, I found myself aligning with the impulsive but still very passionate leader Peter. In my forties, Paul's analytical mind and deep theological truths intrigued me. Now, in my fifties, I find myself becoming more drawn to the Apostle John. These particular reactions come easily. I also am seeking to identify with all the characters in the Bible: men, women, prophets, persecutors, children, the elderly, the physically diseased, and the deserted. I see their human condition and their faith or lack thereof, and I learn how to walk with my heavenly Father.

Saturate the Story with Contemplative Prayer

Learning to hear God's voice necessitates a willingness to listen. Find sacred space for your readings. Seek a place with little or no distractions. My best reading of Holy Scripture is in my office or alone in the backyard at my home.

The ancient rhythm of scripture reading known as *lectio divina* is a wonderful technique of alternating your prayers with reading.[11] It is simple. Choose a text of scripture that you wish to pray. Read until your mind and heart are lifted to the Lord. Be still, and reflect upon what word or phrase stopped you from reading. This will often lead you to a conversation with the Lord about the passage. Sometimes you will simply sit in his presence, ruminating over that passage or quietly saying it. Share with God your discovery. Picture yourself resting in God's loving embrace. Sometimes he will have you return to scripture. Sometimes you know it is time to stop. The only goal of praying the scriptures is to be in the presence of God.

Surrender to What the Spirit of God Is Teaching You

Because the Holy Scriptures are designed for our transformation, we must respond with a steadfast commitment to do the will of God. God is intentionally shaping us so that we can be living in Christ moment by moment and living out Christ to the world. Learning to lead ourselves and others to a higher calling (union with God) must include not only knowing the right thing to do or to be, but also learning how to apply those lessons in everyday living.

Practice the Message You Receive

The courageous follower of Christ responds immediately to the call of God. The conversion story of Augustine of Hippo (CE 354–430), proves the benefit of this practice.[12] Although his mother was a strong Christian, Augustine remained an unbeliever through his early adult years. In his book, *Confessions,* he writes of the deep anguish in his soul about turning his life over to Christ. He heard the voice of a child repeatedly say, "Take up and read." Seeing no children around him or near the neighboring homes, Augustine felt it was the voice of God. He picked up the Book of Romans and decided to read the first passage he saw. The words he found in Romans 13:13–14 changed Augustine forever and his immediate response ultimately changed the course of Christianity. Augustine served faithfully as priest and later bishop in the African city of Hippo, and his writings have been read by millions of Christians even to this day.

TWO GIFTS FROM GOD

Both prayer and scripture are gifts from God. These gifts help us move faithfully through the three stages of spiritual transformation and live in alignment with how God desires us to use our power with fellow humans and the rest of God's creation. They are means of grace to assist us in living out the cross and the towel style of leadership and living "on earth as it is in heaven" (Matt. 6:10).

How do you know that you are moving from one stage to another, drawing closer to that unitive experience because of prayer and scripture? The signs are clear: Your desire for God grows, your complacency about personal holiness is removed, your disordered affections are reduced. You feel greater spiritual detachment and greater love for God and others, and this is seen by your acts of charity in thought, word, and deed.

Like some of the Pharisees and Sadducees in the first century, some people can pray and read scripture without really living to that higher calling. Instead of a relationship with a loving heavenly Father, they want a toy god they can manipulate for their own selfish desires. Although they are religious leaders, they do not know God. They are living with the code of the sword and the shield, not the cross and the towel.

As teachers of God's Holy Word, we really cannot teach what we have not lived. Perhaps that explains the weakness of faith within the Christian church today. If you make a commitment today to see prayers and scriptures with different eyes and a responsive heart, you will never be the same again!

TABLE TALK

In this chapter we saw the importance of prayer and scripture for church leaders. Both prayer and scripture are gifts from God, given to enable us to connect with him. We must devote appropriate time each day to both of God's gifts in order to have a relationship with him and to serve as leaders of his flock. Prayer and scripture fortify us for our ministries. They are the only means by which we can realize our spiritual transformation and find unity with God. Ask yourself how you might strengthen these two vital bonds to God in your own life and ministry.

1. In what ways do you experience contemplative prayer as an intimate conversation with God? Do you have the experience that you are both speaking and listening to God?

2. How do you pray? What are the steps you use to enter into a prayerful state of being?

3. What changes in your behavior or attitude have you noticed when prayer is fully integrated into your daily life?

4. How could you enrich your daily prayer?

5. How would knowledge about your own discipline of prayer be helpful to your congregants?

6. What prayers from scripture or prayer books have been especially meaningful and helpful to you? What are some others that you might explore?

7. How do you use scripture to enhance your daily life?

8. How would you describe the nature of your relationship with scripture? Would you describe this relationship as interactive, continuous, and/or intentionally humble?

9. How would you describe the process you go through when reading scripture? Describe your preparation, your expectations, and your integration (how you allow the stories to "live in you"). What internal processes are at work in you during and after the reading?

10. What changes have you noted about your behavior and attitude as a result of reading scripture as a daily practice?

11. If you were to improve your practice and process of reading scripture, what improvements would you make?

8

Three Vows for a Higher Calling

"Human beings must be known to be loved;
but Divine beings must be loved to be known."
—BLAISE PASCAL

Every person in this world desires to love, to be loved, and to know love. It is a human desire that God has placed in us at birth and will remain in us forever. This desire was demonstrated by Adam and Eve, Abraham and Moses, Mary the mother of Jesus and John, and is, of course, vividly demonstrated in you and me. The heart of all human inspiration is love. Beautiful music, great art, moving literature, and scientific discoveries are the results of that passion to love, to be loved, and to know love.

Why has this desire been placed in all of us? Because God is love, he desires for us to experience that union with him. The Apostle John writes, "Beloved, let us love one another, because love is from God; everyone who loves is born of God and knows God. Whoever does not love does not know God, for God is love (1 John 4:7–8). The higher calling that God desires for all of us is to know and love as we are known and loved by God.

Every aspiration you have had as a church leader is because of that desire. Maybe you gave up a promising career with significant financial reward to attend a three-year seminary program so you could live with less money while working more hours. Why? Love.

Unfortunately, our desire to love, to be loved, and to know love has been distorted. The distortions arrived early, dug deep in our psyche, and have left significant wounds on the surface. The source of the distortions—"the desire of the flesh, the desire of the eyes, the pride in riches"—comes from the impaired world system enflamed by the wiles of the devil (1 John 2:15). The distortions have confused our longings and led us to develop dysfunctional systems to achieve significance and success.

No greater confusion lies anywhere than in our distorted view of money, sex, and power. Business czars have fallen, politicians have resigned, corporations have been fined, police officers have been arrested, and churches have been divided because of the distorted attachments to money, sex, and power. Richard Foster writes, "No topics cause more controversy. No human realities have greater power to bless or to curse. No three things have been more sought after or are more in need of a Christian response."[1]

Clergy scandals over these issues are a weekly occurrence in the news. Deion "Prime Time" Sanders, who played on championship professional football *and* baseball teams, linked power, money, and sex to the three reasons his life was crumbling before he received the Lord Jesus Christ.[2] Tim Keller, the pastor of Redeemer Presbyterian Church in New York City, calls "money, sex, and power" the three "counterfeit gods" in our society.[3]

The ancient church understood these three idolatries. They also understood that these three factors could be a commitment to honor a God-given, healthy desire or an attachment that binds and distorts one. They understood that it wasn't money per se, but that the "love of money that was the root of all evil" (1 Tim. 6:10; Titus 1:7). They understood that sex was not evil. In fact, the early church viewed sex as a gift from God. It was the misuse of sexuality that was evil (Gen. 2:24; Matt. 5:28). They understood that power was a gift from God, but the abuse of power could turn good leadership into evil (Gen. 1:26; Acts 8:19; Rom. 13:1). The distorted healthy desires become greed, lust, and narcissism. They first devour life and then over time destroy life as God intended.

ACCEPTING THE ANCIENT VOWS

The ancient church encouraged its leaders to radically live out the gospel as strong, vibrant witnesses for Christ. Most of the time their values were in direct contrast to the prevailing culture. They would make public professions about how they would order their lives. These promises to God were vows of consecration. Many historians tell us that the monks under Benedict were the first to develop the three public vows in response to the distorted desires of money, sex, and power. However, based on the direct pattern of the life of Jesus, other historians in the church have indicated that this public proclamation and practice existed soon after the time of Christ.

The Roman Catholic Church calls these three vows Evangelical Counsels or Counsels of Perfection. The three vows were designed to liberate the soul from the attachments associated with money, sex, and power. What are these three vows?

- Poverty
- Chastity
- Obedience

Richard Foster calls these ancient vows simplicity, fidelity, and service. These disciplines have provided practical solutions to the world's obsession with money, sex, and power.

These vows are promises made to God that our lives will not be dominated by greed, sex, or power. People in monasteries, friaries, convents, hermitages, and other religious communities have taken these vows in order to follow the Jesus way of living so they can be free to experience the "way of unity" with God. For evangelicals, the tendency is to reject these vows as more "Catholic baggage" added to the grace of God. However, these three virtues provide God's means of grace to liberate church leaders from life's distractions and help form a believer into Christlikeness.

Most spiritual mystics would recognize these vows as opportunities for "detachment" so that you can grow in freedom as a person. The purpose of taking these vows is not to stop loving the things and people of this world, but to love them as God designed—under the rule of Christ and through the power of the Holy Spirit.

The scriptural passage often used to support the teachings on the "evangelical virtues" is found in Matthew 19. The reference to chastity appears at the beginning of the chapter after the Pharisees questioned Jesus about divorce. His disciples asked if it would be better not to marry. But he said to them, "Not everyone can accept this teaching, but only those to whom it is given" (Matt. 19:11).

Let's take a look at the vow the church has taken from this text—the vow of chastity.

THE VOW OF CHASTITY

The vow of chastity (or fidelity) taken by the early monks was a choice to identify with Christ in the expression of love for all people rather than entering a conjugal marital relationship with another human being. This vow was in direct response to the distorted view that to be fully human one must be sexually active.

There was no question that most of the earliest Christian leaders were married (Mark 1:30; 1 Cor. 7:8; 1 Cor. 9:5; 1 Tim. 3:2). In AD 110, Ignatius writes to Polycarp, encouraging the priests and their wives to live faithfully with each other in body and soul.

In AD 306, a local church council in Elvira, Spain, attempted to mandate celibacy for priests. However, bishops meeting in the recognized Council of Nicaea in AD 325 decreed that "too heavy a yoke ought not to be laid upon the clergy; that marriage and married intercourse are of themselves honorable and undefiled."[4] It was not until the fourth century that church leaders (bishops, priests, and deacons), were required to abstain from conjugal relations during certain periods of time (Council of Carthage, AD 387).[5] Eventually, mandated celibacy became the norm for bishops and priests in the Roman Catholic Church. Today, the Eastern Orthodox Church mandates celibacy for bishops but not for priests. The recent sex abuse scandals within the Roman Catholic Church have led many to question mandated celibacy for the clergy.

It is not the purpose of this chapter to discuss the pros and cons of this practice but to see how important the vow of chastity is for married and single clergy seeking to walk in union with God. It should be noted that sex abuse scandals exist among married clergy in Protestant denominations as well.

That members of the clergy violate this vow does not nullify its importance for church leaders today. A vow of chastity is not easy, but it is necessary for every believer.

Chastity is the proper restraint of the sexual gift God has given all human beings. God, out of his loving goodness, created all of us with sexual desires. Unfortunately our sexual desires, disturbed by personal wounds and magnified by self-rule, can find unhealthy ways of expression. When egged on by the world's systems, the descent into sexual disorder becomes self-destructive (Rom. 1:14–26).

Our spirituality and our sexuality have been designed by God from the beginning to be in alignment. Our sexuality, male and female, is made in the image of God. Today we see our sexuality in terms of our genitals, instead of seeing our entire being, including our sexuality, in the context of a spiritual person. The result is sexual obsessions, human trafficking, pornography, adultery, promiscuity, and issues related to sexual identity. The Vatican, in its teaching on adultery, states, "Chastity means the successful integration of sexuality within the person and thus the inner unity of man in his bodily and spiritual being."[6] It is a good definition that promotes fidelity to God, others, and yourself.

What Does Chastity Mean for Church Leaders?

First, chastity affirms our sexuality as a gift from God. Sex was never designed to depersonalize another human being or to be viewed in dark, dirty, and unwholesome ways. Chastity recognizes that sex is a beautiful and wonderful expression of married love that affirms both procreation and mutual pleasure. Our sexuality is healthy.

Chastity also affirms our apprenticeship as Christ-followers as we develop the cardinal virtue of temperance. Chastity affirms that we do not trust human relationships for our security but God alone. The vow of chastity recognizes our ongoing development in the discipline of detachment. It allows us to make space for God.

Additionally, chastity affirms our commitment to be faithful to God within our current state of life. Chastity recognizes that singleness is a gift of God for some but not for all. Chastity acknowledges that some have been married, but through the divorce or death of their spouses are no longer married. It recognizes that some struggle with disordered and undisciplined affections. Chastity confirms that, regardless of our status or condition, the with-God life is the life God has designed for us.

Furthermore, chastity affirms the covenant of marriage as lifelong loving expression of fidelity between "a man and a woman" who become "one flesh." Chastity recognizes that the marriage covenant is a beautiful picture of Christ's faithful love for his bride, the Church.

Finally, chastity affirms mutual respect and well-being of the other made in the image of God. Chastity acknowledges that all human beings, regardless of age, gender, status in life, or color of skin, are to be revered as God's creation. Chastity affirms the second commandment, "You shall love your neighbor as yourself."

A vow of chastity demands that the follower of Christ avoid even entertaining the possibilities associated with sexual temptations. Lust for another has a bewitching effect upon our senses and quickly can darken our hearts and minds, filling them with ungodly fantasies and memories. No wonder the spiritual writers, all in unified agreement, give two great counsels: avoid the temptation of curiosity and use prayer.

Avoid the Temptation of Curiosity.

St. Bernard of Clairvaux calls curiosity the first step Lucifer uses to transform a humble life with God to a life of devil-like pride. Bernard writes, "He increases your interest while he stirs up your greed. He sharpens your curiosity while he prompts your desire. He offers what is forbidden and takes away what is given. He holds out an apple and snatches away paradise."[7]

Clergy have the same technological tools as the average person. The Internet can provide us hours of self-entertainment in all kinds of sensual vices. Curiosity can drive pastors away from their holy calling, causing them to dwell on what life would be like with that attractive congregant, seeing what the commotion is all about on pornography websites, or even watching popular but seductive television shows or movies. Some clergy tell me that they need to be aware of these sites, movies, or programs, so that they can help others in their spiritual walk. I wonder what impact their research has had on their spiritual well-being? Such things are easier to avoid than to cure.

Pray!

Fulfilling the vow of chastity is impossible without prayer. Prayer is the definitive tool to help us in our walk with God. Prayer allows us the freedom to be transparent before God. Prayer gives us a way to secure empowerment from the Holy Spirit and live a life of chastity. Church leaders who have fallen from their calling through impurity universally have indicated that they lacked a vibrant prayer life. So pray!

Here is a prayer that Thomas Aquinas, one of the greatest theologians, left us in his quest for chastity:

Dearest Jesus!

I know well that every perfect gift, and above all others that of chastity, depends upon the most powerful assistance of your providence, and that without you a creature can do nothing. Therefore, I pray that you defend, with your grace, the gifts of chastity and purity in my soul as well as my body. And if I have ever received through my senses any impression that could stain my chastity and purity, I ask you, who are the supreme Lord of all my powers, to take it from me, so that I may with a clean heart advance in your love and service, offering myself chaste all the days of my life on the most pure altar of your divinity. Amen.[8]

THE VOW OF OBEDIENCE

The second vow also has roots in Matthew 19. The vow of obedience is a choice to identify with Christ, as he was completely obedient to the Father in all things. We choose to seek the common good over personal desire and make a commitment to live under the authority of our legitimate superior in the faith. This vow offers God the greatest of all sacrifices, our personal will.

The little children depicted in Matthew 19 were seen by many of the spiritual fathers of the church as an example of filial obedience. Children in the first century were completely dependent upon their parents for their well-being. They lived a life of trust, responding to their parents' direction even when asked to do something difficult. They trusted their parents even when they did not understand because their parents had their best interest in mind.

Jesus taught the disciples about prayer using the important relationship between a trusted father and a dependent child. Jesus, in ending a dispute among his disciples on which of them was the greatest, brought a little child before them as a living illustration on how to enter the kingdom of heaven. Jesus said, "Assuredly, I say to you, unless you are converted and become as little children, you will by no means enter the kingdom of heaven" (Matt. 18:3). The child again is completely dependent upon the Father's character for his care. If it is true with imperfect parents and their children, it is more so with a perfect God and us.

Power is designed to liberate people to become as God has designed them. When power becomes evil, it seeks to dominate, control, manipulate, and maneuver people to its own end. In a world obsessed with power, a call for obedience is necessary for all church leaders. This vow of obedience is a virtue that seeks common good over personal interest. This vow of obedience is a vow of service to God and his Church.

In the Church, the recognized leaders have a responsibility to not use their God-given authority in self-serving ways. The Book of Titus describes it as not being "self-willed" (Titus 1:7). Timothy describes it as "not quarrelsome" or being "puffed up with pride" (1 Tim. 3:3, 6). In 3 John, the apostle writes about a church leader named Diotrephes, "who loves to have preeminence" (3 John 9).

All those seeking Holy Orders in the apostolic traditions of Roman Catholic, Eastern Orthodox, and Anglican churches take the vow of obedience. As an ordained priest, I am required to obey my bishop and other ministers who might have authority over me and my ministry. Many evangelical churches, often known as "free churches," do not have these particular requirements in their ordination ceremonies. The independent spirit within evangelicalism has created a strong entrepreneurial quality among its leadership that has led many to start great ministries for the Lord but also has left them answerable to no one. Some pastors within those traditions have also told me they have felt lonely serving without supportive accountability and being deprived of an experienced shepherd for guidance. Most compensate by intentionally seeking other pastors in their denomination or professors from their seminaries for spiritual guidance.

What Does the Vow of Obedience Affirm for Church Leaders?

The vow of obedience affirms our choice to live in compassionate service for the sake of others. It affirms our choice to engage the world with the cross and the towel instead of the sword and the shield. The tools we use and the attitude we demonstrate are as significant as our achievements.

The vow of obedience affirms our choice to let go of our personal power in order to harness the true power from God. This vow helps us recognize the constant efforts we make to secure our own desires instead of the godly characteristics of contentment and peace.

Our vow of obedience affirms our choice to live in humility with patient and obedient hearts toward those who have been placed in authority over us. It acknowledges that we might disagree with the decisions made, and even recognize the imperfections of the person in authority, but seek to live for the greater good God desires for us.

Our vow of obedience affirms our choice to become servant

leaders in order to inspire, equip, and encourage others we influence. Our vow of obedience is a gift God provides us in order to model consistent Christlikeness before others, so they can see holy consecration in action.

Like chastity, obedience requires prayer. I have taped the following prayer in my Bible for almost two decades now. I say it daily in my prayers, and it has been a great help to me during my journey of obedience. I recommend it to you.

We are no longer our own, but thine.
Put us to what thou wilt, rank us with whom thou wilt.
Put us to doing, put us to suffering.
Let us be employed by thee or laid aside for thee,
Exalted for thee or brought low by thee.
Let us have all things, let us have nothing.
We freely and heartily yield all things
To thy pleasure and disposal.
And now, O glorious and blessed God,
Father, Son, and Holy Spirit,
Thou art ours, and we are thine. So be it.
And the covenant, which we have made on earth,
Let it be ratified in heaven. Amen.[9]

THE VOW OF POVERTY

The third vow for church leaders also has its roots in Matthew 19 when Jesus told the rich young man, "If you wish to be perfect, go, sell your possessions, and give the money to the poor, and you will have treasure in heaven" (Matt. 19:21).

The rich young man, an ideal church member, just walked

away from Jesus when he heard this. He was a respected pillar of the community, perhaps even a committed Pharisee, who simply wanted an answer to a genuine question about eternal life. He confirms that he has followed the law. But Jesus moves him from external conformity of the law to truly examining his heart by exposing the counterfeit god in his life—money. Because of his recognized piety, the rich young ruler undoubtedly gave alms to the poor. After all, it would be considered a sacred duty. However, he wouldn't stop worshipping the true ruling force in his life—his possessions.

The Bible says that the disciples were "greatly astonished" at the interchange and wondered if salvation was really possible. It is through this passage that the Franciscan and Benedictine monks took seriously the call of poverty.

St. John of the Cross writes about how temporal goods weaken our soul for God when they become attachments to our passion. Once the attachment is nailed to our passion, the object worshipped undermines our freedom to freely love God, others, and ourselves. He writes, "People should not rejoice over riches, neither when they possess them nor when their neighbor possesses them, unless God is served through them."[10]

The vow of poverty helps us to avoid backsliding, a "blunting of the mind," increasing leniency to ignore spiritual disciplines and eventual covetousness. The very memory loss of God means a new god—greed—is enthroned in your soul (Col. 3:5). It is counterintuitive to the sensual mind, but the very practice of taking the vow of poverty only will increase a purer joy in receiving temporal goods. We see that spiritual truth exhibited in children who have every toy imaginable but do not really appreciate them. In contrast, we see that same truth when a child who has nothing experiences a greater joy in one temporal good received than a child who has everything.

The vow of poverty means a detachment of the desires that imprison and distort our souls. God is not against wealth. Many of his greatest servants were men of wealth, including Abraham, Isaac, Jacob, and King David. But their wealth was not their god. The followers of Jesus, many of whom supported Jesus financially, were men and women of wealth. The vow of poverty focuses church leaders on the kingdom, trusting God to provide for their well-being, and not allowing the allure of increased possessions to deter their trust in God. As Hebrews 13:5 states, "Keep your lives free from the love of money, and be content with what you have; for he has said, 'I will never leave you or forsake you.'" According to the Apostle Paul, true contentment comes in trusting the providential loving rule of God in our economic circumstances (Phil. 4:12).

Many who are reading this book are struggling with meeting their financial commitments right now. Some have paid or will be paying institutions thousands of dollars yearly for an education for a Master of Divinity degree. In the ministry, many times the pastor's spouse is also working just to provide for the daily family needs. Resentment can develop when a pastor and family witness extravagant spending by parish members who ignore the pastor's financial plight. There is no question that this kind of behavior is intolerable in God's kingdom. As the scripture clearly states, the teacher within a congregation is worthy of "double honor." But consider the words of the Apostle Paul to his beloved Timothy, who is pastoring a church in Ephesus:

... those who want to be rich fall into temptation and are trapped by many senseless and harmful desires that plunge people into ruin and destruction. For the love of money is a root of all kinds of evil, and in their eagerness to be rich some have wandered away from the faith and pierced themselves with many pains. (1 Tim. 6:9–10).

What Does Poverty Affirm for Church Leaders?

The vow of poverty affirms your ability to do justice fairly and not to be swayed by people with financial means. The vow of poverty indicates that you cannot be bought because Christ has already bought you. The vow indicates that you will show no preferential treatment.

The vow of poverty also affirms your clarity of purpose in seeking God's kingdom and his righteousness. It means you seek to obey God in all things, find fulfillment in God for all things, and love God above all things. The vow affirms your modesty in spending and extravagance in giving. The vow of poverty affirms that God is trustworthy, and his creatures trust in his provision. You reject anxiety, seek simplicity, and receive goods gratefully.

The vow of poverty makes space available to love God and serve God in order to advance his kingdom. People who seek riches are preoccupied with efficiency and obsessed with results. This takes away time and energy from the calling God has given them and, more importantly, distorts their souls.

Finally, the vow of poverty affirms that financial wealth is designed for us to give away generously and joyfully to all those in need. This vow affirms our need to provide for not only our family, but also others as God leads us.

The vow of poverty is a spiritual discipline that helps us

overcome any deformity of the soul that comes from "all kinds of greed" (Luke 12:15). You choose to be detached from possessing things so you can be liberated to follow Christ. Choosing to identify with Christ and the poor rather than the distorted desires of a materialistic culture can be the most liberating, consecrating action you have ever taken.

HOW CAN I DO IT?

Incorporating the three vows into your life will require a spiritual transformation. You might be wondering how this is possible.

During my doctoral studies at Fuller Seminary, I had a wonderful opportunity to study under Dallas Willard. In his book, *Renovation of the Heart,* he describes why spiritual transformation rarely is successful: "Imagine a person wondering day after day if he is going to learn Arabic or if he is going to get married to a certain person—just waiting to see whether it would happen. That would be laughable. But many people live this way with respect to their spiritual transformation."[11]

The steps of spiritual transformation, according to Dallas Willard, are based upon vision, intention, and means. The vision demands an understanding of what is the ideal, the intention demands a commitment to certain values, and the means are the spiritual practices necessary to increase our capacity for God. (In the next chapter, you'll learn more about the seven practices every church leader must have.)

As usual, Dallas Willard is absolutely spot on! Spiritual transformation requires a choice. The ancient church used the word *asceticism*, which comes from the Greek word *askeo* (to exercise). Our will needs to be *exercised* through various spiritual disciplines so that we can move our will from the willfulness of control to willingness to surrender all to Jesus. The exercise is not the source of freedom in Christ; it is simply the means to achieve the vision and the intention of that liberation. What God is after most of all is your heart, not new behavioral practices, nor deep insights.

The disciplines that create a consecrated heart are contained in the vows of poverty, chastity, and obedience. How do you do it?

Remember the Vows You Already Have Made

Take a moment to review the vows you have already made in life. Marriage, parenthood, ordination, and installation service come easily to my mind as some of the vows often made by a church leader. If possible, secure a copy of the ordination vows you made and prayerfully review them. How similar are they to the vows of poverty, chastity, and obedience?

During my ordination into the priesthood, the bishop outlined my tasks as a presbyter in God's Church:

- Proclaim by word and deed the gospel of Jesus Christ

- Fashion my life in accordance with the gospel

- Love and serve young and old, strong and weak, and rich and poor alike

- Preach God's forgiveness to penitent sinners

- Pronounce God's blessing, share the administration of Holy Baptism, and celebrate the mysteries of Christ's Body and Blood (*Book of Common Prayer,* pp. 531–532)[12]

Willingly Choose Daily to Live According to Those Vows

After remembering the vows you have made before God and others, thank the Lord Jesus for the trust he has placed in you for the lives of others. Confess the times you have violated those vows in life, and ask God to have mercy upon you and forgive you of your sins.

As if it was yesterday, I remember when Bishop Gethin Hughes asked me if I was willing to live in obedience, chastity, and poverty of heart in order to serve God and his Church. He also asked me if I was willing to be diligent in the two gifts God provides all ministers of the gospel: prayer and scriptures. He encouraged me to live in union with God and asked God to give me the grace and power necessary to live accordingly.

Since that very personally moving service of consecration before God, I have looked at the vows I made during the ordination. I have found myself thanking God for that day and confessing to God my limitations. But every day, I make a choice intentionally, prayerfully, and willingly to live according to those vows made during my ordination. It is not that my heart does not struggle at times with the attachments associated with the love of money, sex, and power. They might never be removed on this side of life, but they can be delivered through our awareness, God's grace upon us, our vision for God's union, and our desire through the disciplines for deliverance.

Three Vows for a Higher Calling

Seek His Heart Above Everything Else

Take a moment to review your life in the light of God's desire for you. Many of you, like the biblical rich young ruler, are extremely talented and enormously respected. Those characteristics are particularly conducive to self-deception. We hide, rationalize, deny, and repress our true attachments associated with money, sex, and power. Until we see the ugliness of our current state of self-deception, we will never move from here to there. We must love One above any other, including our spouse, children, and ministry. The church must never be our "mistress." We must intentionally seek Jesus's heart. We must desire above anything else to have one heartbeat with the Savior and the mind of Christ.

Live in Gratitude for the Calling on Your Life

The ministry is the greatest calling in the world. As the greatest calling, it is also one of the most difficult callings God provides. However, God takes great joy in calling us, and we must take great joy in our calling. Take a look at the names in the church directory; spend time with each person, recalling their journey with God. Think about how God used you to help them in that journey. Smile as you remind yourself of the good times you have experienced with them —the "ah ha" moments they received from your ministry. Gratitude is a characteristic of kingdom children. As pastors, a thankful heart goes a long way in dealing with the long hours of ministry. A heart filled with gratitude will open itself up to be loved, be in love, and become a bearer of God's love.

Just before I was vested according to the Holy Order of Priests, Bishop Gethin prayed over me the words that appear below. It is my prayer for you as you open yourself up to be loved, be in love, and be the bearer of love for God and his kingdom:

May this servant exalt you, O Lord, in the midst of your people; offer spiritual sacrifices acceptable to you; boldly proclaim the gospel of salvation; and rightly administer the sacraments of the New Covenant. Make him a faithful pastor, a patient teacher, and a wise councilor. Grant that in all things he may serve with reproach, so that your people may be strengthened and your Name glorified in all the world. All this we ask through Jesus Christ our Lord, who with you and the Holy Spirit lives and reigns, one God, forever and ever.

And all the people responded: Amen![13]

TABLE TALK

In this chapter we reviewed the three ancient church vows of chastity, poverty, and obedience. We saw how these vows serve to hold church leaders close to God by disciplining our selfish human nature and how prayer plays a crucial role in helping us to stay true to our vows. Being held bound by these vows reminds us to respect human sexuality, renounce worldly possessions, and honor God's authority so that we can better serve others in our ministry. Think about which of these three vows represents your greatest challenge in your personal life and ministry.

1. Think through the passages of scripture and write down the names of those individuals who were influenced negatively because of their attachment to money, sex, and power. In which area do you most struggle in your own life?

2. Have you read about or do you know those who have violated these vows? What factors led them to not honor their vows?

3. The violation of these vows can be done in "thought, word, or deed." In which of these three areas do you have the greatest struggle?

4. What steps can you take to help yourself take these vows and apply them to your everyday life?

5. How do your finances affect your attitude? How about your spouse? What ways can you learn contentment concerning your financial state? What is God teaching you about money?

6. Pornography is an increasingly difficult issue for pastors whom I counsel. What steps can you take to remove yourself from these images? In what ways does the Word of God help? What particular passages stand out for you about the way you need to think?

7. How do the vows of poverty, chastity, and obedience help a pastor be more effective as a shepherd of God's flock? Look at the life of Jesus. What freedoms did he have in his ministry because of these practices? How did people relate to him because of these practices? Note that the enemies of Jesus were people who were obsessed with money, sex, and power.

9

Becoming a Servant Leader

"And this is eternal life, that they know you the only true God,
and Jesus Christ whom you have sent."

—JOHN 17:3

I used to be a certified bubble wrap pastor, leading a church of people who were also covered in bubble wrap. My unseen bubble wrap permitted me to hear from others and speak to others. Their bubble wrap allowed them to hear my words but not listen to them. Although our bubble wrap was invisible, it insulated us from the really difficult stuff associated with love, like hurt, betrayal, and dishonesty. The bubble wrap permitted us to dismiss relationships easily, slander others covertly, and be unreachable and untouchable. It let us hide from each other.

At ministry or work, the bubble wrap helped us become more professional than personal. With all the new technologies, the bubble wrap also helped us become more efficient. We knew how to do things better now with our bubble wrap. Unfortunately, our bubble wrap made us forget *why* we were doing those things.

In this closing chapter, I want to share with you the seven

key practices of a servant leader, one who no longer wants to be a bubble wrap pastor but a shepherd of God's flock. Indeed, that kind of servant leader can truly be an ambassador and herald of the kingdom of God.

Leadership is an art, not a science. And pastoral leadership is one of the most difficult of all the leadership arts. This kind of leadership, when done well, takes godly character, truthful communication, gentle chemistry, and competency development, all within a church culture that is both willing and reluctant. This kind of leadership is not about the sword and the shield so often exhibited in the world today. This kind of leadership is more powerful because the power comes from God. This leadership is the cross and the towel. This requires a true servant leader.

The previous chapters were designed to inspire, equip, and encourage you to know this one truth above all truths: Leaders must lead themselves before they can truly lead others. Leaders must lead themselves to a higher calling before they can ever expect their congregants to follow the way of union with God. The unitive experience with God, fully practiced, is the fulfillment of all desire within humanity. Most Christians, unfortunately, believe "eternal life" or "kingdom life" or "salvation" is about the future—when we die. Did they get that idea because we church leaders do not have a unitive experience with God?

ACT STRATEGICALLY

Servant leaders seek lasting change for their faith community. They think and act strategically about the mission of God instead of focusing on providing organizational relief to the self-serving complaints of some very vocal congregants.

The scriptures speak to us about God's story of his mission through his people who engage in this world for the sake of all. The only way God has chosen to bring blessing to all the nations of the earth, ultimately renewing his whole creation, is through his chosen people. It is a remarkable thought that God chooses to use us in order to achieve his purpose. God has a mission, which means God's people have a mission to be a light for all the peoples of the earth to see the glory of God (Isa. 40:5). The Church, along with its leaders, ultimately exists for the sake of others. It is through Jesus that God is fully revealed. It is in Jesus that we see the pinnacle of God's story in the world and the pledge that all that has been promised will be fulfilled (Rev. 7:9–10).

This kind of strategic focus allows a servant leader to see all of humanity, including the Church, as created in the image and likeness of God (Gen. 1:26–27). As humans, we are spiritual beings made in the image of God. The image of God is not just simply a classical definition of intellect, emotion, and will. Of course, we can have limited self-determination, which gives us the ability to choose good or evil. But it is more than that. God creating us in his image is the very reason we have a need to love, be loved, and to be bearers of love. This image we bear speaks to us of our life accountability, our incredible value as individuals, our desire for relationships, and our equality with fellow human beings. Unfortunately, our fallen condition has distorted our perspective about God. We have created self-made idols, reducing our worth as human beings by making ourselves tools for efficiency. We have objectified relationships for our own pleasures and ignored our responsibility to care for every aspect of God's creation (Gen. 3:15–17; Rom. 1–2; 3:23; 8:20–28).

Yet in spite of our marred condition, the image of God

remains in every human being. The Church, as a witnessing light to all the nations, has a responsibility to actively engage in the world by providing educational, physical, emotional, and spiritual development in the name of Christ.

Churches become increasingly influential when they serve the needs of this world without trying to control the institutional power structure. The issues of human sexual trafficking, AIDS/HIV, poverty, slavery, illiteracy, hunger, gangs, domestic violence, and unjust economic, political, cultural, and religious practices are some areas where the servant leader must inspire, equip, and encourage God's flock to act according to God's desire for healing.

How does the mission of God play out strategically for the servant leader? Ask yourself the following questions:

- Because the church budget is a moral document, in what ways is my church budget a reflection of the mission of God for a humanity that is made in the image of God?

- What are the three greatest needs within my city or town where my church could be a blessing from God and a light to others? Have I asked the city officials?

- What intentional learning experiences am I providing for my church so members can be inspired, equipped, and encouraged in engaging with God's mission in the world?

- How much of my pulpit teaching surrounds helpful guidelines in coping with life versus ways to live in union with God and in union with his mission?

- How much activity am I asking a church member to do inside the buildings of the church instead of being the church in the world? Is it achieving the mission of God?

The calling for pastors is not to recruit people for positions within the church in order to provide organizational relief. Instead, pastors need to inspire, equip, and encourage God's people for God's vision in a world he loves. It is God's mission that we need to get on with in the Church.

ENCOURAGE RELATIONSHIPS

Servant leaders seek transformation for their faith community. They inspire, equip, and encourage intimate relationships instead of dependent relationships within the congregation. Pastors face a great temptation to be the center of congregational life. However, when a church becomes personality driven, it no longer has Christ on the throne. It is energized more by the charisma of the pastor than by the power of the Holy Spirit. Personality-driven churches create congregations that are dependent upon the pastor instead of communities that are growing together in intimate relationship with God and one another. Here are some characteristics of a personality-driven church that creates dependent relationships. Do any of them sound familiar?

- Attendance significantly goes down when the senior pastor is not present.

- Visual displays of the senior pastor are featured on websites, advertisements, and other venues of church visibility.

- The pastoral staff experiences significant turnover.

- Worship service focuses on the personality and gifts of the pastor instead of being a participative worship experience where gifts from the parish are used.

Servant leaders serve the congregation well when they encourage intimacy and experience with God and fellow believers. This is the essence of the meaning of the word *fellowship*. Genuine intimacy provides trust and creates goodwill. Intimacy allows the congregation to take risks and be vulnerable and authentic. Intimacy creates a bonding of friendship when the stressors of life make it difficult to engage with one another. Read the epistles by the Apostle Paul, and you see the importance of intimacy for the people of God:

- Be devoted to one another in brotherly love. Honor one another above yourselves. (Rom. 12:10)

- Live in harmony with one another. (Rom. 12:16)

- Love one another. (Rom. 13:8)

- Stop passing judgment on one another. (Rom. 14:13)

- Accept one another. (Rom. 15:7)

- Instruct one another. (Rom 15:14)

- Greet one another with a holy kiss. (Rom. 16:16; 1 Cor. 16:20; 2 Cor. 13:12)

- Serve one another in love. (Gal. 5:13)

All of these passages correspond to the words of Jesus when he said to his disciples on the last night before his crucifixion, "A new command I give you: Love one another. As I have loved you, so you must love one another. By this all men will know that you are my disciples, if you love one another" (John 13:34–35).

The early church achieved intimacy, as you read in Acts 2, "They devoted themselves to the apostles' teaching and to the fellowship, to the breaking of bread and to prayer. Everyone was filled with awe, and many wonders and miraculous signs were done by the apostles. All the believers were together and had everything in common. Selling their possessions and goods, they gave to anyone as he had need. Every day they continued to meet together in the temple courts. They broke bread in their homes and ate together with glad and sincere hearts, praising God and enjoying the favor of all the people. And the Lord added to their number daily those who were being saved" (Acts 2:42–47).

Intimacy is created in small groups, when we gather together for a meal or celebrate the presence of Christ in the Eucharist. Intimacy is created when there is community prayer and sharing of resources and when there is laughter and tears. Intimacy is created through service in the community. Servant leaders do not need to be the center of these activities. Instead, they should be a voice that encourages these gatherings of the saints in fellowship together.

PERSEVERE PATIENTLY

Servant leaders persevere with a nonanxious presence filled with prayer, knowing that reactions, resistance, and rumors are evidence that God is at work. A good example of this state of mind was my father in-law, who built sport-fishing yachts for a living. He loved the sea, and as an experienced boater, he knew that overcoming the winds and currents without the right kind of power would be fruitless. I would see him carefully position his boat for docking, using the right amount of power to work with the prevailing winds and currents instead of working against them. Again and again, I was impressed that Bob so calmly could maneuver a 110-foot sport fishing yacht so easily into a relatively tight spot.

Pastoral leadership is a little like boating. You have to know the prevailing winds and currents of your congregation. Churches usually have two types of crises. Someone in the congregation causes the first type of church crisis. These usually start small like a complaint but move rapidly within the congregation through rumors and speculative scenarios. Usually the pastor has to prayerfully consider the options. Does this call for a command decision, consensus decision, consultation decision, or a convenience decision? Most of the time in this scenario, pastors get in trouble only when they make a command decision where it would have been more appropriate to consider a consensus or consultation decision as an option.

The second type of crisis is far more difficult. This type of crisis is caused by the way leaders respond to resistance within the congregation. Most of the time, pastors will inadvertently create more disorder by becoming anxious about events and will respond in nonhealthy ways to deal with the problem. This anxiety comes through self-righteous anger, poorly timed words, and accusations of evil intent against individuals. The key to successful pastoral leadership is a nonanxious presence in the midst of resistance, rumors, and reactions.

Practicing the presence of God moment by moment through contemplative prayer certainly will reduce your anxiety. The Apostle Paul provides an example in his response to Euodia and Syntyche, two women at the church in Philippi. They were in conflict with one another and were causing a disruption within the church. They were respected church leaders and served with Paul on the mission field. You can imagine that the congregation was already taking sides by discussing who did what, who started it, and so on.

Paul's nonanxious response to their crisis provided clarity to the congregants. He writes, "whatever is true, whatever is noble, whatever is right, whatever is pure, whatever is lovely, whatever is admirable—if anything is excellent or praiseworthy—think about such things. Whatever you have learned or received or heard from me, or seen in me—put it in practice" (Phil. 4:8–9 NIV).

Notice the counsel of Paul. Focus with joy upon God because he is present. Respond with gentleness to others and prayers to God. Think about the things that are beautiful and positive in life, and be willing to put them into practice. Follow my attitude in the midst of a crisis, and you will do well. Then you will experience a powerful peace because God is one with you.

Because life happens, resistance will happen in the Church.

The way servant leaders handle themselves will go a long way in resolving the issues.

INSPIRE RESPONSIBILITY

Servant leaders inspire personal responsibility and community responsibility instead of encouraging a victim mentality within the congregation. Some people are true victims in this world. They need us to help them by the grace of God to overcome and be made well. But our society has created a victim mentality by advocating individual rights instead of responsibility. This kind of thinking has invaded the Church. A victim mentality within a congregation will create alienation from one another, an entitlement of privileges, the necessity of excessive pastoral attention, a tendency to blame orientation, and a lack of contentment in life.

All of us can tell stories about the injustices we have suffered at the hands of another. My dear friend, Keith Matthews, is the chair of the pastoral ministry department at the Azusa Pacific University School of Theology. He invited me to spend the weekend at an extensive workshop with him and others called Discovery. Led by Daniel Tocchini and Jean Jobs, the seminar is a three-day transformational interaction with God and others that creates a healthier way of thinking about life. You literally repent of your victim mentality and have the freedom to choose responsibility. Then you can look at your betrayal stories in a new way.

For example, several decades ago I wrote a book on workplace violence that changed the course of my life. The book was used as a textbook for Fortune 100 companies and universities that were concerned about the increasing incidents of violence in the workplace. The United States Postal Service hired my organization to train their leaders and most of their 750,000 employees in how to handle emotionally charged individuals. In the early 1990s, I was traveling 200 to 250 days a year to meet with clients. I was burned out and sold my business to some friends. Trusting them, I accepted no guarantee or long-term payments. I was willing to work part-time for them, so I could concentrate more on writing and getting involved with the church. After six months, they quit paying me. They kept my phone line open with my voice on it telling people that I was traveling even though I no longer worked for them. I was betrayed. The courts ruled in my favor two years later. Then, these "friends" simply closed the offices and started another business a few miles away. I felt like a victim.

But the truth of the matter was that I needed to take responsibility for what had happened. The responsible act—if not for me, then for my family—would have been to secure personal guarantees. The responsible action would have been to do proper diligence on the partners associated with my friends. Even though the new buyers were clearly wrong, I still had responsibility.

Servant leaders rarely talk about how the Church is victimized by society. However, they do talk about the responsibility we have as individuals and as a community to partner with God in being a blessing to this world. The poor counselor or spiritual director is one who provides empathy without questioning responsibility. God wants his people to take responsibility for his world.

INVEST IN MOTIVATED PEOPLE

Servant leaders invest in motivated people instead of adapting to troubled members of the flock. When I teach in churches or Christian colleges, I receive more pushback on this practice than any other. When they quote to me the Parable of the Lost Sheep in Matthew 18 and say that our "Father in heaven is not willing that any of these little ones should be lost," I agree with them. I also point out the passage is about how we are to model our lives as children before God with complete trust and dependence. It tells us that we are to welcome children, respect them, and to model godly behavior for them. It also tells us that we should not give up on our children.

All of this is true, but it doesn't speak of our priorities in dealing with adults. There are better biblical examples that show how shepherds prioritize their time around the motivated. Jesus invested his time with motivated, not disinterested people. He invested three years with the disciples. He invested his time with the many followers who responded to his message. Jesus, even though he loved the rich young man, allowed him to choose another direction. He invested his time with Zacchaeus. His parable often called the Prodigal Son is a story of a rebellious son who returns to his father (Luke 15:11–20). The father deeply loved him, but he did not go after him. Only when the son was motivated to return did the father run to meet him.

A servant leader always loves and is always available to a responsive heart. Discipline may be needed for correction, but when a troubled individual acts defiant, it is time to invest in the motivated instead. Too many times, the servant leader will ignore motivated people who want to learn and grow and instead concentrate on the uninterested and unrepentant. That is unfortunate.

Seek to inspire, equip, and encourage the motivated, and you will have many who can help you with the flock. Spend most of your time with the complainers, whiners, judgers, and apathetic, and you will demotivate the motivated within your flock. The motivated are the ones who need the most of your time, talent, and treasures.

ACKNOWLEDGE PRE-EXISTING PROBLEMS

Servant leaders perceive interpersonal conflict as a revelation of pre-existing problems within the Church instead of seeing these conflicts as the source of the problem. Conflict reveals the character of the individual and the congregation. It provides an accurate assessment of the current spiritual condition. Interpersonal issues within a congregation are usually symptoms of a greater problem within. Effective pastoral leaders learn how to not only manage the symptoms, but also diligently investigate the pre-existing source.

Emotional processes within churches have been reinforced through decades. That is one reason why certain churches have a repeated history of splits, moral issues, and intense conflicts. Many times, it is far easier to start a new church than to try to reverse a pre-existing problem when the people have demonstrated over several generations that they are not interested in changing.

The crisis within the Anglican Communion concerning the Episcopal Church is an example of how interpersonal conflict reveals a pre-existing problem instead of being the source of the problem. Most of the orthodox believers within the Episcopal

Church took some type of action in response to the consecration of an openly gay bishop from New Hampshire in 2003. Shortly thereafter, a conference held in Dallas, Texas, brought together conservative laity and clergy. Eventually, the result was the formation of the Anglican Church in North America in 2009.

The presenting problem was homosexuality. However, homosexuality was not the pre-existing interpersonal conflict. Some will tell you the problem was the ordination of women, but that again was simply a symptom of a deeper problem within the Episcopal Church. Finally, many orthodox believers within the Episcopal Church will tell you that the source of the problem was directly related to the differing views about the authority of scripture. Of course, both the progressives and the conservatives agree they have differing views related to scriptural authority. But even that was not the source of the interpersonal conflict.

These issues reveal the pre-existing problems within the Church. The pre-existing problem, manifested for generations in the Episcopal Church in the United States, was delayed adolescence. The Episcopal Church, from the very beginning to now, has manifested many of the traits associated with this stage of life: a bent to challenge authority, the rejection of advice from older leaders, fervent individualism, a fascination with extremes, an openness to change, a willingness to take risks, momentous mood shifts, and a constant exploration of new options. No wonder the modern-day Episcopal movement is preoccupied with sex. It is simply an adolescent institution gone wild with freedom.

Now the response within the Episcopal Church by the conservatives manifested some characteristics of adolescence as well. As a delegate for the formation of the new Anglican Church in North America, I witnessed firsthand the above characteristics among the orthodox clergy and the laity. By the grace of God, the Holy Spirit prevailed over this new movement but not before destroying some of the trust among the Anglican partners.

In a situation like this, servant leaders need to step back from the symptoms and prayerfully look for the source, the root of the issue. It is only then that true healing can take place.

LIVE FOR ONE

Servant leaders live for the applause of the One as opposed to the applause of many. Servant leaders respond to the direction of the chief shepherd, Jesus Christ. Like Jesus did in his earthly ministry, pastors must listen intently to God's voice and behave accordingly. Their primary responsibility is to take care of God's flock.

The Bible often refers to leaders as shepherds. For example, God is the chief shepherd of his flock (Ps. 23, 80:1). Jesus described himself as the Good Shepherd in John 10:11–18. God expected his chosen leadership to function as shepherds to the people of Israel (2 Sam. 5:2). God also dealt harshly with those shepherds who acted out of self-interest and abused their power (Ezek. 34). Peter instructs the presbyters/elders to shepherd the flock of God by being willing examples and servants of Jesus Christ (1 Peter 5:4). Paul instructs the elders in Ephesus to shepherd the church of God by protecting them from the wolves who distort the truth (Acts 20:28).

The shepherd was the customary metaphor for a ruler in the ancient world because they were responsible for taking care of the flock. The shepherd provided nourishment by leading his flock to pastures and water. The shepherd also protected them from wild animals. He kept a count of his sheep and gave special attention to the littlest lambs.

The shepherd can never be a rancher. A rancher is the equivalent of a modern-day executive overseeing an operation. There is a deep intimacy to the relationship between shepherd and sheep. A shepherd needs sheep, and the sheep need a shepherd.

The shepherd understands authority and responsibility. The final practice for all servant leaders is that their lives must focus on the chief shepherd and live only for his applause, not for those of the cynics or the congregants.

CONCLUDING THOUGHTS

Lasting change takes a heavenly vision. Faithful shepherds are willing to see that God provides heavenly vision for his flock. They are willing to invest their time and talent in their congregation, not to build an institutional church, but to develop and equip an incarnational people. Teaching others to live moment by moment as an apprentice of Jesus, with the goal of oneness with God on earth as it is in heaven, takes time. Resistance is guaranteed. Many in the Church may prefer the easier life of dating Jesus. They define Christianity by what people believe and not by how they practice their faith. But they will miss the fulfillment of all their desires by not having a spiritual marriage with Jesus.

Don't be surprised if attendance goes down because you have moved your Sunday morning service from an entertainment model to one that engages the soul. God's power, the only true power, will be exhibited among the people of God.

Remember that the early church leaders also had to make

a decision about choosing lasting change versus organizational relief. Examples abound:

- In facing moral duplicity within the newly formed Christian community, the Apostle Peter could have ignored the deceptive lie of Ananias's and Sapphira's claim that they had given all that they had in the selling of their property for the church. If Peter had remained silent, he would have chosen to participate in their little secret. By doing so, he would have provided organizational relief to a potential confrontation in the church where people may undoubtedly have taken sides. However, Peter, as a leader in the church, openly confronted the couple by stating to them and all who could hear, "You have not lied to us but to God" (Acts 5:1–11). The Apostle Peter wanted lasting change for the church community in Jerusalem, not just temporary organizational relief.

- In facing the divisions within the church described in 1 Corinthians 1, Paul could have ignored the competitive pettiness in the church over the favorite leader. That would have been a choice for temporary organizational relief. Instead, he chose lasting change. He knew this was an issue of hearts looking to leaders for their fulfillment instead of to God. Paul pointed out that favoritism was not God's way but our imperfect tendency to turn leaders into celebrities. He then proceeded to talk about the mature way of living life where God alone is the focus.

- Finally, the last example is the acceptance within the Corinthian church concerning sexual immorality. The Apostle Paul could have again been silent because the church did not seem to have an issue with it. In fact, the Corinthian church looked upon their acceptance as an act of compassion and love. Paul was not interested in organizational relief; he was interested in holiness. He was interested in the Corinthian church living in Christ and living out Christ—in essence, to be the people of God, the Body of Christ, and the temple of the Holy Spirit. The Apostle Paul dealt openly with the sin. After the confession of sin, Paul then restored the repentant parties into full fellowship, teaching the congregation about not only sin, but also forgiveness (1 Cor. 5).

In all these examples, lasting change necessitated inside-out transformation based on principles that motivate the heart. For us, too, lasting change allows our future in Christ to intrude into our present life with him. When we adopt a lasting change mentality, we work toward becoming a Christlike community, seeking God with all our heart.

The journey starts today. Note the time. Your new life, seeking that unitive experience with God, is the very most important item on your agenda right now. Seek it, thirst for it, and receive it!

TABLE TALK

In this chapter we looked at practical ways to improve as servant leaders in the Church. The actions of the early church leaders show that they were willing to forego worldly applause and to overlook personal hardships in order to build the kingdom of God. Whatever the cost, they chose lasting change over temporary comfort. Consider the ways you might focus more of your energy on achieving a more Christlike community within your own ministry.

1. Anne Rice is not the only person who has distanced herself from the Church. Do you know others? What are the reasons they have provided to you? Are the reasons theological ones, or do they concern how the Church relates to the world?

2. To you, is love more of an action, feeling, or knowledge about someone? What factors tell you that you are loved? Loved by God? Loved by your children? Loved by your spouse? And loved by your friends?

3. Have you ever met a bubble wrap Christian? What were the signs? How did those signs make you feel as a person?

4. What percentage of your time as a pastor or church leader is spent on the mission of God versus providing organizational relief within the church? Has your congregation or your leadership board ever done a study on this subject? Review your financial statements at the church. How is the budget a reflection of the mission of God? What steps can you take to fulfill your real calling?

5. Besides your spouse, who is your closest friend at church? What characteristics mark that relationship? Who in your leadership team do you have the most difficulty relating to? Why? What can be done to build a closer relationship?

6. Within your church, what intentional practices can you use to avoid a personality-driven church?

7. Do you think like a victim? Share a story with another about being a victim of someone's actions. Then share the same story making yourself responsible. How does the story differ? What did you learn?

8. Out of the seven practices, which one speaks most clearly to you about the changes you need to make in your approach to leadership?

Epilogue

There is only one measurement standard for Jesus in ministry; it is holiness. There are two primary means of grace. They are gifts God provides to us so that we can reach those standards: prayer and the Word of God. There are three vows every church leader must make within his heart to avoid the addictive idolatries of money, sex, and power that distort our souls from that unitive experience with God: the vows of poverty, chastity, and obedience. If we capture the vision God has for us, if we have honest intentions to achieve that vision, and if we use the right means to discipline ourselves in honoring our intentions, we will have the fulfillment of all desire as a servant of the Lord.

This is self-differentiated leadership. This kind of leadership has the capacity to stand firmly in Christ in an often intense, emotional system like the Church and lead followers to love, be in love, and become bearers of love.

I no longer seek to be a rancher of God's people, but a shepherd of their souls. It is not that I have reached any milestones of pastoral perfection, but I have given up the fake images I presented before others and the false idols I had deemed necessary for pastoral success. I want to be a pastor who loves, is in love, and is a bearer of love to others.

Every soul must undergo a deep purification in order to experience fully a unitive life with God. This purification is found in the crucified life. I love how Eugene H. Peterson expresses this passage in *The Message:*

> *I tried keeping rules and working my head off to please God, and it didn't work. So I quit being a "law man" so that I could be God's man. Christ's life showed me how, and enabled me to do it. I identified myself completely with him. Indeed, I have been crucified with Christ. My ego is no longer central. It is no longer important that I appear righteous before you or have your good opinion, and I am no longer driven to impress God. Christ lives in me. The life you see me living is not "mine," but it is lived by faith in the Son of God, who loved me and gave himself for me. I am not going to go back on that. (Gal 2:19–21)[1]*

To God be the glory!

Endnotes

INTRODUCTION

1. Anne Rice, *Christ the Lord: Out of Egypt* (New York: Ballantine Books, 2008), 333.
2. "Q & A: Anne Rice on Following Christ Without Christianity," *Christianity Today*, accessed August 24, 2010, http://www.christianitytoday.com/ct/augustweb-only/43-21.0.html.

PART I

1. William H. Willimon, *Pastor: A Reader for Ordained Ministry* (Nashville, TN: Abingdon Press, 2002), 280.

CHAPTER 1

1. Archaeological Study Bible (Grand Rapids, MI: Zondervan Press, 2005), 1757.
2. Mark 8:34 (NRSV).
3. John 13:12–15 (NRSV).

CHAPTER 2

1. Phil Cooke, "A Shocking Response From Many Major TV Ministries," *The Change Revolution,* November 23, 2009, accessed December 9, 2009, http://www.philcooke.com/direct_mail_response.

2. Ibid.

3. Ibid.

4. Church of England, "Addressing the Clergy," accessed December 9, 2009, http://www.cofe.anglican.org/info/addressingtheclergy.html.

5. Orthodox Christian Information Center, "Clergy Etiquette," accessed December 9, 2009, http://www.orthodoxinfo.com/praxis/clergy_etiquette.aspx.

6. WikiHow, "How to Address Catholic Clergy," accessed December 9, 2009, http://www.wikihow.com/Address-Catholic-Clergy.

7. Tony Baron, *The Art of Servant Leadership: Designing Your Organization for the Sake of Others* (Tucson, AZ: Wheatmark 2010), 11.

CHAPTER 3

1. Rita Healy, "A Mega-Scandal for a Mega-Church," accessed December 23, 2009, http://www.time.com/time/nation/article/0,8599,1554388,00.html. Haggard resigned as pastor.

2. Catholic News Service/U.S. Conference of Catholic Bishops 2007, American Catholic.org, accessed on December 23, 2009, http://www.americancatholic.org/news/clergysexabuse/.

3. Ibid.

4. David Johnson and Jeff VanVonderen, *The Subtle Power of Spiritual Abuse* (Ada, MI: Bethany House, 2005), 24.

5. Archaeological Study Bible (Grand Rapids, MI: Zondervan Press, 2005), 1654.

6. Evangelical Catholic Apologetics, "How Many Protestant

Endnotes

Denominations Are There?," accessed July 14, 2010, http://www. bringyou.to/apologetics/a120.htm.

7. David Kinnaman and Gabe Lyons, *UnChristian: What a New Generation Really Thinks About Christianity...and Why It Matters* (Grand Rapids, MI: Baker Books, 2008), 26–27.

CHAPTER 4

1. U.S.–Canada Power System Outage Task Force, "Final Report on the August 14, 2003 Blackout in the United States and Canada: Causes and Recommendations," accessed May 14, 2010, https:// reports.energy.gov/.

2. Wikipedia, "Northeast Blackout of 2003," accessed September 20, 2010, http://en.wikipedia.org/wiki/Northeast_Blackout_of_2003.

3. David E. Fitch, "Our Definition of Success," *The Great Giveaway: Reclaiming the Mission of the Church from Big Business, Parachurch Organizations, Psychotherapy, Consumer Capitalism, and Other Modern Maladies* (Grand Rapids, MI: Baker Books, 2005), 27–46.

4. Willow Creek Community Church, "Teaching Pastors," accessed May 14, 2010, http://www.willowcreek.org/teachingpastors.

5. Andrew Louth, ed., *Early Christian Writings: The Apostolic Fathers*, rev. ed. (London: Penguin Classics, 1987), 103.

6. Veli-Matti Karkkainen, *An Introduction to Ecclesiology: Ecumenical, Historical, and Global Perspectives* (Downers Grove, IL: IVP Academic, 2002), 23.

7. Mirsolav Volf, *After Our Likeness: The Church as the Image of the Trinity* (Grand Rapids, MI: Wm. B. Eerdmans Publishing Company, 1997), 27.

8. "Meet the Real Reverend Billy Graham—He Is Not the Person Whom You Thought You Knew!," accessed July 9, 2010, http://www. cuttingedge.org/news/n1355.cfm; "Report Says Young Evangelicals Calling Rick Warren/Bono Role Models," accessed July 9, 2010,

http://www.lighthousetrailsresearch.com/blog/?p=360&zoom_highlight=bono.

9. "Weblog: As the World Prays, Falwell and Robertson Blame ACLU, Gays, and Others for 'Deserved' Attack," *Christianity Today,* accessed May 19, 2010, http://www.christianitytoday.com/ct/2001/septemberweb-only/9-10-52.0.html.

10. "Pat Robertson: Haiti 'Cursed' Since Pact with the Devil," *Christianity Today*, accessed May 19, 2010, http://blog.christianitytoday.com/ctliveblog/archives/2010/01/pat_robertson_h.html.

PART II

1. John C. Maxwell, *The 360 Degree Leader: Developing Your Influence from Anywhere in the Organization* (Nashville, TN: Thomas Nelson, 2006), 283.

CHAPTER 5

1. *The Westminster Larger Catechism: A Commentary* (Philipsburg, NJ: P & R Publishing, 2002), 3.

2. *The New Interpreter's Dictionary of the Bible,* vol. 4 (Nashville, TN: Abingdon Press, 2008), 828–836.

3. Ibid., 828–836.

CHAPTER 6

1. *City Slickers*, accessed July 22, 2010, http://www.quotegeek.com/index.php?action=viewcategory&categoryid=694.

2. Eugene H. Peterson, *The Message*: The Bible in Contemporary Language, Numbered Edition. (Colorado Springs, CO: NavPress, 2005), 1545.

3. Dallas Willard, *The Kingdom Life: A Practical Theology of Discipleship*

and Spiritual Formation, Alan Andrews, gen. ed., (Colorado Springs, CO: NavPress, 2010), 23.

4. Ibid., 85.

5. Ralph Martin, *The Fulfillment of All Desire: A Guidebook for the Journey to God Based on the Wisdom of the Saints* (Steubenville, OH: Emmaus Road Publishing, 2006), 11–12.

6. Henri J. M. Nouwen, *The Return of the Prodigal Son: A Story of Homecoming* (New York: Doubleday, 1994), 68–69.

7. Willard, *The Kingdom Life,* 35.

CHAPTER 7

1. Wikipedia, "English versions of the Nicene Creed in current use," accessed August 25, 2010, http://en.wikipedia.org/wiki/English_versions_of_the_Nicene_Creed_in_current_use.

2. Henri J. M. Nouwen, *In the Name of Jesus: Reflections on Christian Leadership* (New York: Crossroad Publishing Company, 1992), 32–33.

3. Ibid.

4. Ibid.

5. Ibid., 43.

6. Bill Hybels, *The Power of a Whisper: Hearing God, Having the Guts to Respond* (Grand Rapids, MI: Zondervan, 2010), 16.

7. St. Therese Martin of Lisieux, *The Story of a Soul,* trans. John Clarke, OCD, (Washington, DC: ICS Publications, 1996), 82–83.

8. St. Francis de Sales, *Introduction to the Devout Life,* trans. John K. Ryan (New York: Image Books, 1989) 82.

9. Archaeological Study Bible, 1771.

10. Eugene H. Peterson, *Eat This Book: A Conversation in the Art of Spiritual Reading* (Grand Rapids, MI: Wm. B. Eerdmans Publishing Co., 2009), 18.

11. Father Luke Dysinger, O.S.B., "How to Practice the Lectio Divina: A

step-by-step guide to praying the Bible," accessed August 23, 2010, http://www.beliefnet.com/Faiths/Christianity/Catholic/2000/08/ How-To-Practice-Lectio-Divina.aspx.

12. Philip Schaff, ed., "The Confessions and Letters of Augustine, with a Sketch of His Life and Work," *Nicene and Post-Nicene Fathers,* 1st ser., vol. 1, (Peabody, MA: Hendrickson Publishers Inc., 1999), 127–128.

CHAPTER 8

1. Richard Foster, *The Challenge of the Disciplined Life: Christian Reflections on Money, Sex, and Power* (New York: Harper & Row, 1985), 1.

2. Deion Sanders, *Power, Money, & Sex: How Success Almost Ruined My Life* (Nashville, TN: Thomas Nelson, 1999), 123.

3. Timothy Keller, *Counterfeit Gods: The Empty Promises of Money, Sex, and Power, and the Only Hope That Matters* (New York: Dutton, Penguin Group, 2009), 205.

4. Christian Classics Ethereal Library, "The Canons of the 217 Blessed Fathers who assembled at Carthage," accessed August 23, 2010, http://www.ccel.org/ccel/schaff/npnf214.xv.iv.iv.iv.html.

5. Ibid.

6. "Part Three: Life in Christ, Section Two: The Ten Commandments, Chapter Two 'You Shall Love Your Neighbor As Yourself' Article 6, The Sixth Commandment," *Catechism of the Catholic Church,* accessed August 23, 2010, http://www.vatican.va/archive/ccc_css/ archive/catechism/p3s2c2a6.htm.

7. St. Bernard of Clairvaux, *Selected Works,* trans. G.R. Evans, The Classics of Western Spirituality (New York: Paulist Press, 1987), 125.

8. St. Thomas Aquinas, "Prayer for Chastity," accessed August 23,

Endnotes

2010, http://courageman.blogspot.com/2007/06/chastity-prayer.html.

9. *Celtic Daily Prayer Book: Prayers and Readings from the Northumbria Community* (New York: HarperOne, 2002), 43.

10. St. John of the Cross, *The Collected Works of St. John of the Cross,* vol. 3 of *Ascent of Mount Carmel,* trans. Kieran Kavanaugh, OCD, and Otilio Rodriguez, OCD (Washington, DC: ICS Publications, 1991), 296–297.

11. Dallas Willard, *Renovation of the Heart: Putting On the Character of Christ* (Colorado Springs, CO: NavPress, 2002), 84.

12. *1979 Book of Common Prayer Reader's Edition* (New York: Oxford University Press, USA, 2008), 531–532.

13. Ibid., 534.

EPILOGUE

1. Eugene H. Peterson, *The Message: The Bible in Contemporary Language,* New Edition ed., (Colorado Springs, CO: NavPress, 2007), 1605.

Bible Resources

Archaeological Study Bible. Grand Rapids, MI: Zondervan Press, 2005.

The ESV Study Bible, English Standard Version. Wheaton, IL: Crossway Bibles, 2008.

The Holy Bible, New International Version. Grand Rapids, MI: Zondervan Bible Publishers, 1978.

The New Oxford Annotated Bible, New Revised Standard Version. New York, NY: Oxford University Press, Inc., 1994.

Peterson, Eugene H. The Message: The Bible in Contemporary Language, Numbered Edition. Colorado Springs, CO: NavPress, 2005.

The Spiritual Formation Bible, New Revised Standard Version. Grand Rapids, MI: Zondervan, 1999.

Recommended Reading

1979 Book of Common Prayer, Reader's Edition. New York: Oxford University Press, USA, 2008.

Baron, Tony. *The Art of Servant Leadership: Designing Your Organization for the Sake of Others.* Tucson, AZ: Wheatmark, 2010.

Blessed Raymond of Capau. *The Life of St. Catherine of Siena.* Charlotte, NC: TAN Books and Publishers, 2009.

Catechism of the Catholic Church, "Part Three: Life in Christ, Section Two: The Ten Commandments, Chapter Two 'You Shall Love Your Neighbor As Yourself' Article 6, The Sixth Commandment," http://www.vatican.va/archive/ccc_css/archive/catechism/p3s2c2a6.htm.

Celtic Daily Prayer Book: Prayers and Readings from the Northumbria Community. New York: HarperOne, 2002.

Chan, Simon. *Liturgical Theology: The Church as Worshipping Community.* Downers Grove, IL: IVP Academic, 2006.

Christian Classics Ethereal Library, "The Canons of the 217 Blessed Fathers who assembled at Carthage," http://www.ccel.org/ccel/schaff/npnf214.xv.iv.iv.iv.html.

Dysinger, Father Luke O.S.B. "How to Practice the Lectio Divina: A step-by-step guide to praying the Bible," http://www.beliefnet.com/Faiths/Christianity/Catholic/2000/08/How-To-Practice-Lectio-Divina.aspx.

Fitch, David E. *The Great Giveaway: Reclaiming the Mission of the Church from Big Business, Parachurch Organizations, Psychotherapy, Consumer Capitalism, and Other Modern Maladies.* Grand Rapids, MI: Baker Books, 2005.

Foster, Richard. *The Challenge of the Disciplined Life: Christian Reflections on Money, Sex, and Power.* New York: Harper & Row, 1985.

Hunter, Todd D. *Giving Church Another Chance: Finding New Meaning in Spiritual Practices.* Downers Grove, IL: IVP Books, 2010.

Hybels, Bill. *The Power of a Whisper: Hearing God, Having the Guts to Respond.* Grand Rapids, MI: Zondervan, 2010.

Johnson, David and VanVonderen, Jeff. *The Subtle Power of Spiritual Abuse.* Ada, MI: Bethany House, 2005.

Recommended Reading

Karkkainen, Veli-Matti. *An Introduction to Ecclesiology: Ecumenical, Historical, and Global Perspectives.* Downers Grove, IL: IVP Academic, 2002.

Keller, Timothy. *Counterfeit Gods: The Empty Promises of Money, Sex, and Power, and the Only Hope That Matters.* New York: Dutton, Penguin Group, 2009.

Kinnaman, David and Lyons, Gabe. *unChristian: What a New Generation Really Thinks About Christianity...and Why It Matters.* Grand Rapids, MI: Baker Books, 2007.

Law, William. *A Serious Call to a Devout and Holy Life.* Peabody, MA: Hendrickson Publishers, 2009.

Louth, Andrew, ed. *Early Christian Writings: The Apostolic Fathers,* revised ed. London: Penguin Classics, 1987.

Martin, Ralph. *The Fulfillment of All Desire: A Guidebook for the Journey to God Based on the Wisdom of the Saints.* Steubenville, OH: Emmaus Road Publishing, 2006.

Maxwell, John C. *The 360 Degree Leader: Developing Your Influence from Anywhere in the Organization.* Nashville, TN: Thomas Nelson, 2006.

Nicene and Post-Nicene Fathers, Volume 1: "The Confessions and Letters of Augustine, with a Sketch of His Life and Work," First Series. Philip Schaff, ed. Peabody, MA: Hendrickson Publishers Inc., 1999.

Nouwen, Henri J. M. *The Return of the Prodigal Son: A Story of Homecoming.* New York: Doubleday, 1994.

Nouwen, Henri J. M. *In the Name of Jesus: Reflections on Christian Leadership.* New York: Crossroad Publishing Company, 1992.

Payne, Leanne. *Listening Prayer: Learning to Hear God's Voice and Keep a Prayer Journal.* Ada, MI: Baker Books, 1999.

Peterson, Eugene. *Answering God: The Psalms as Tools for Prayer.* New York: HarperOne, 1991.

Peterson, Eugene. *Eat This Book: A Conversation in the Art of Spiritual Reading.* Grand Rapids, MI: Wm. B. Eerdmans Publishing Co., 2009.

Rice, Anne. *Christ the Lord: Out of Egypt.* New York: Ballantine Books, 2008.

Sanders, Deion. *Power, Money, & Sex: How Success Almost Ruined My Life.* Nashville, TN: Thomas Nelson, 1999.

Sanford, Agnes. *Behold Your God.* Austin, MN: Macalester Park Pub Co., 1979.

St. Augustine of Hippo. *The Confessions of St. Augustine: Modern English Version.* Ada, MI: Revell, 2008.

Recommended Reading

St. Francis de Sales. *Introduction to the Devout Life.* John K. Ryan, translator. New York: Image Books, 1989.

St. John of the Cross, *The Collected Works of St. John of the Cross, Book III: Ascent of Mount Carmel.* Kieran Kavanaugh, OCD, and Otilio Rodriguez, OCD, translators. Washington, DC: ICS Publications, 1991.

St. Therese Martin of Lisieux, *The Story of a Soul,* John Clarke, OCD, translator. Washington, DC: ICS Publications, 1996.

Volf, Mirsolav. *After Our Likeness: The Church as the Image of the Trinity.* Grand Rapids, MI: Wm. B. Eerdmans Publishing Company, 1997.

The Westminster Larger Catechism: A Commentary. Philipsburg, NJ: P & R Publishing, 2002.

Willard, Dallas. *Renovation of the Heart: Putting On the Character of Christ.* Colorado Springs, CO: NavPress, 2002.

Willard, Dallas, contributing author, Alan Andrews, gen. ed. *The Kingdom Life: A Practical Theology of Discipleship and Spiritual Formation.* Colorado Springs, CO: NavPress, 2010.

Willimon, William H. *Pastor: A Reader for Ordained Ministry.* Nashville, TN: Abingdon Press, 2002. Includes St. John Chrysostom's writing, "The Glory of the Priesthood."

World Christian Encyclopedia: A Comparative Survey of Churches and Religions in the Modern World. New York: Oxford University Press, USA, 2001.

Wright, N.T. *Jesus and the Victory of God.* Minneapolis, MN: Fortress Press, 1996.

Wright, N.T. *The New Testament and the People of God.* Minneapolis, MN: Fortress Press, 1992.

Young, Brad H. *Meet the Rabbis: Rabbinic Thought and the Teachings of Jesus.* Peabody, NJ: Hendrickson Publishers, 2007.

About the Author

Rev. Canon Dr. Tony Baron

Tony Baron holds a double doctorate in psychology and theology and currently serves as president of Servant Leadership Institute at Datron World Communications, Inc., headquartered in Vista, California. A respected author, Dr. Baron's two most recent books are entitled, *The Art of Servant Leadership: Designing Your Organization for the Sake of Others* and *The Cross and the Towel: Leading to a Higher Calling.* An adjunct faculty member in leadership at several graduate schools, Dr. Baron teaches, trains, and consults with corporate and church leaders around the world on how to live for the sake of others. An ordained Anglican priest and canon within the Anglican Mission, Dr. Baron is board certified in forensic medicine, is a diplomate of the American Board of Psychological Specialties, and has served as past regional director within the Order of St. Luke Healing Ministry. Dr. Baron currently serves as lead teaching pastor at The Way Christian Fellowship in Vista, California (www.findtheway.org).

About Servant Leadership Institute

Servant Leadership Institute is a resource created to serve you and to help you build an organization that is determined to make a positive difference in the world. We not only link like-minded servant leaders with each other, but we help them with strategic vision, training, and resources. Here are some ways SLI can serve you:

- Servant Leadership Summit—An annual two-and-a-half-day conference to envision and equip servant leaders with greater leadership gifts and skills. Presented live in San Diego, this conference is designed to increase the leadership effectiveness of organizational leaders worldwide. Two special modules on the various aspects of servant leadership are provided. They feature nationally known speakers in the corporate and church world.

- Servant Leadership Resources—Trusted and field-tested publications, training manuals, newsletters, and field guides that can be used by your trainers or serve as library resources within your corporation or church.

- Conference Speaking and Training Opportunities—Dr. Tony Baron, Datron owner Art Barter, and a talented array of servant leader speakers are available for your organization. Training classes can be provided to your organization as needed.

- Servant Leadership Consulting—Our team can provide long- or short-term mentoring for those interested in becoming a better servant leader. Our experienced team walks with you through the process of transformation.

Servant Leadership Institute is committed to serving you. If you are an organization with limited financial means, Datron World Communications is willing to provide scholarships to qualified candidates so that your future servant leaders can be inspired, equipped, and encouraged to make a difference in the world.

For more specific information about Servant Leadership Institute, please call (760) 597-3796 or visit our website, www.forthesakeofothers.com.

CPSIA information can be obtained at www.ICGtesting.com
Printed in the USA
LVOW040005080612

285209LV00002B/1/P